Business Risk Workaholism

Dr Ulrike Emma Meißner

Business Risk Workaholism

Management challenges and action guidelines for professional practice

PETER LANG

Bibliographic Information published by the Deutsche Nationalbibliothek
The Deutsche Nationalbibliothek lists this publication in the Deutsche Nationalbibliografie; detailed bibliographic data is available online at http://dnb.d-nb.de.

Library of Congress Cataloging-in-Publication Data
A CIP catalog record for this book has been applied for at the Library of Congress.

ISBN 978-3-631-76634-7 (Print)
E-ISBN 978-3-631-76635-4 (E-PDF)
E-ISBN 978-3-631-76636-1 (EPUB)
E-ISBN 978-3-631-76637-8 (MOBI)
DOI 10.3726/b14596

Peter Lang – Berlin · Bern · Bruxelles · New York · Oxford · Warszawa · Wien

This publication has been peer reviewed.

www.peterlang.com

To Emily, Emilian, Holger and my mother

Foreword

'*To have my problems acknowledged*', is what a participant in this study would have wished for from his employer in regard to his own affliction with workaholism. The increasing social awareness of this 'phenomenon' has been a positive development over the last ten years. The wish quoted above, however, is representative of reality in the corporate world. There, the acknowledgement of workaholism as a serious problem an employee might face, is not the focus of attention to this day and is, indeed, largely and resolutely blocked out. The fact that this illness often circulates in a conglomerate of personal predisposition, operational framework and management behaviour does not attract attention in operational practice or operational health management. It clearly becomes apparent how the consequences of workaholic behaviours for businesses are addressed from an economic and human resources perspective and that they imply a high risk potential. Workaholism research in German speaking countries, to date, has focussed mainly on the psychological aspects of workaholism. My 2005 study (Meissner 2005), dealing with the human resources risks of workaholism for companies, from an economic point of view, still constitutes one of the first research papers to do so. It examined the indications of workaholism from a business perspective; test subjects were employees in human resources departments. At that time, it showed that all indications of the disease were apparent in businesses and, therefore, it stressed the importance of adequate human resources risk management to identify the workaholism risk within companies. To further explore the human resources issues within the framework of empirical research, I developed a study comparable to the one in 2005, which, however, addresses the target group of 'workaholics' directly. For the first time in the German-speaking world, those affected evaluated themselves with regard to behavioural characteristics of workaholism and commented on the development and promotion respectively of workaholism through the company. The results of the current study will be compared with the 2005 study and interpreted. The objective of this research is to verify to what extent those afflicted with workaholism can confirm those indications of workaholism already identified by human resources managers in the 2005 study. This is followed by a human resources risk analysis, as well as by a depiction of concrete human resources instruments businesses may implement to actively tackle this risk area in practice.

This empirical survey has been made possible thanks to the members of *Workaholics Anonymous*, who, by answering the questions, have made a vital contribution to workaholism research. I would like to take this opportunity to sincerely thank them for their willingness to participate in this study!

I would like to especially thank my family, without whom this book would not have been possible. My daughter I thank from the bottom of my heart for her untiring willingness to voluntarily cook for the family. Her dishes were always extraordinarily delicious. My son I thank for his relentless motivation through hugs and his encouraging interest in the book, although, being 11 years old, he might be a little young to fully understand it. Finally, I would like to thank my husband and sparring partner for his continuous attention, his interest, his illuminating insights and our discussions, as well as for his patient tech support!

It should be mentioned, that this book is a translation of the German version: Unternehmensrisiko Arbeitssucht, published by Peter Lang Verlag, Germany, 11/2017.

I hope that I may, with this book, make a further contribution to ensuring that workaholism be perceived and acknowledged by society and by businesses as an existential illness that can afflict people and employees. From a business perspective, not only aspects of welfare must thereby be taken into account. Rather an active approach to this human resources risk area will contribute to avoiding significant monetary ramifications (loss of benefits/chances as well as arising costs) or even existential consequences for business; a situation from which both employees and companies will profit equally.

Upper Moutere, March 2018

Contents

List of figures

List of tables

List of abbreviations

DSM-V	Diagnostic and Statistical Manual of Mental Disorders V.
ICD-10-GM	International Classification of Diseases, 10. Revision, German Modification
KonTraG	Law on corporate control and transparency (Gesetz zur Kontrolle und Transparenz im Unternehmensbereich = KonTraG)
SEA	Scale for the recording of work relatedness (Skala zur Erfassung von Arbeitsbezogenheit = SEA)
WAI	Work-Ability-Index
WART	Work Addiction Risk Test
WHO	World Health Organisation

1 Introduction

The phenomenon that is workaholism has undergone a shift and today carries a different weight in society and business from what it did only ten years ago. Back then, workaholism was often associated with high professional performance pressure, but also with career and prestige. People usually jokingly said they were a 'workaholic'. It was perceived positively in society and accepted. Increasing education, however, has led to a shift in perception. If the topic workaholism is brought up within a company or human resources management meetings, immediately the discussion centres on symptoms of the condition and the negative impact it has on those affected and the companies they work for. This is a clear indication for an increasing acceptance of workaholism as a problem and even as an illness. This changed perception also documents itself in the increasing numbers of Workaholics Anonymous groups, which have representations in 28 German speaking cities thus far.

A serious analysis of workaholism in the public as well as the commercial sector, however, has failed to materialise. It is being discussed in society and information is available, but no action is being taken. In medicine, workaholism is, to date, not a medically recognised condition, although more and more clinics have actively incorporated the issue into their therapeutic concept.

The particularity of this form of addiction is that, even though workaholism is the problem of an individual, it should be seen in the context of a social and corporate environment, as it is lived out and is triggered in these environments.

Acting in a professional environment, thus, gains a special significance.

The ever-advancing technological possibilities and changes in work organisation contribute to the boundaries between work and leisure being increasingly blurred. Teleworking from home, being constantly available via mobile phone or the internet or flexible working hours can promote workaholism. An operational framework has been established, which enables the employee to quickly and flexibly respond to requests from superiors. There is a big temptation to make phone calls at the weekend or while away on holiday, documenting to the outside world, how seemingly indispensable the employee is to the company. Therefore, if there is a problem around work addiction, one should place a focus on operational frameworks to consider and recognise the responsibility that they could be an addiction cause or promoter. At the same time, this might be seen as a reason why workaholism is disclaimed as an operational problem and why research also, so far, has only rudimentarily addressed this issue from an operational perspective.

The qualitative empirical findings in regard to the causes, characteristics, symptoms, types and progression of the addiction were gathered from the psychological care for those affected (see for example Robinson, Mentzel, Berger) as well as through the provision of consulting services to companies, in which workaholic staff were employed (see for example Wilson-Schaef, Fassel). In addition, Poppelreuter conducted and published a larger empirical study in Germany in the form of interviews and questionnaires, focussing on surveying workaholics and non-workaholics (see Poppelreuter 1996, p. 248 ff.). In his survey, he followed the symptoms of the addiction and determined four types of workaholism.

Moreover, the following works have been published in Germany:

Schneider 2001:
In his 2001 theoretical thesis with the University of Würzburg, Schneider developed an instrument for the measurement of workaholism (scale for the recording of work relatedness (SEA)). This scale consists of 20 items attributed to workaholism which are to be answered by selecting Yes/No. Each selection of a Yes-answer is seen as an indicator for workaholism and counted as one point. The probability of the presence of workaholism is calculated by adding up the points.

Jungkurth 2005:
Jungkurth analysed whether the questionnaire developed by Spence and Robbins (1992) was also suitable to depict workaholism in Germany and could be used as a measuring tool.

Voigt 2006:
In her study, Voigt focussed on the question of whether a workaholic role model in childhood increases the risk of the addiction occurring in adulthood, and if workaholics show manifestations of certain character traits.

Sandjaja 2007:
Sandjaja discussed the scientific standard of the topic of workaholism at the time, while putting emphasis on diagnostics, stages, types, symptoms and the effects of workaholism.

Städele 2008:
In her study, Städele pursued the objective of identifying health and psychological impairments suffered by workaholics and of examining the concurring

occurrence of workaholism and a compulsive personality style, as well as of a compulsive personality disorder. As a measuring tool, she used Schneider's workaholism scale.

Bielert 2009:

Bielert focussed on the handling of workaholism in workplace health promotion and preventative measures.

Matthey 2011:

In his empirical study, Matthey took an in-depth look at the question whether workaholism is especially prevalent among journalists, while consulting Schneider's workaholism scale.

Vicario 2013:

Vicario, following up Matthey's study, and in her empirical study, delved further into the question whether workaholism is especially prevalent among helping professions and for that purpose also consulted Schneider's workaholism scale.

The effects of workaholism on business operations and human resources are, to this day, only marginally mentioned in the established literature. The only analysis expressly focussing on human resources was conducted in 1984 by Richter, Gößman and Steinmann, who identified workaholism as a human resources problem. Richter's research showed up some consequences with respect to employee selection, caring and development.

Hence, the 2005 study is, to date, the only investigation in the German speaking world addressing the operational and human resources risks and the impact of this illness on businesses.

The following case study will demonstrate the effects of the addiction:

The Head of IT of a corporation with approx. 20,000 employees was a workaholic. In the beginning, the addiction was not noticed; the IT department performed well and was productive. After a while the number of employees handing in their notice increased. The corporation's Managing Directors took notice, but did not react. It was after a fundamental decision made at highest corporate level, to modernise and replace the hopelessly outdated core IT system, that the problems began: The decision model presentations requested by management were not delivered in a timely manner. When questioned, the Head of IT stated that the models still needed improvement and had been handed back by him to the employees. When the employees were asked, they voiced a high level of frustration, as the content of the models was good, but the Head of IT did not accept them. Thereby, the processes were delayed by several months, staff turnover increased, and more and more employees became sick. After a delay of one year, the implementation of the new system began. During the changeover, specialist knowledge was still required for the continued existence of the company, internally developed and only partially documented legacy systems, which, due to the resignations, were no longer available within the company. The only person who still had the specific expertise was the Head of IT himself, and he was absent for six months during the changeover period due to being diagnosed with burnout. Even after his return, his capacity to work was only limited. The project suddenly stagnated and was delayed by more than a year. The costs caused by the delay (hiring additional interim IT specialists, post-documentation of the old software, and longer project duration) well and truly reached seven figures. An assessment of the loss suffered through the delayed introduction of the new system and the associated significant delay in the introduction of faster processes and improved transparency was never carried out.

As Figure 1 shows, workaholics, from an operational point of view, are, to a certain extent, of positive use for a company. Their high level of motivation often comes with a high level of productivity and is highly appreciated by companies. In this phase (Phase 1A), workaholics seem very effective and efficient. They are rewarded by the company with recognition and prestige and successfully further their careers. From the company's point of view, they are the 'best employees'! At a later time, every workaholic will, however, reach a point (Phase 1B), when he[1] is still being effective and making a positive contribution, but the efficiency is beginning to suffer and those affected compensate for the declining efficiency, for example with additional time at work in the form of overtime or weekend work. During this phase, companies typically ignore the associated problems. After all, this is still their best employee, and they are willing to generously overlook any anomalies. If the utility curve falls into negative figures in Phase 2, the company incurs costs or loss of use. In this phase, workaholics work neither effectively nor efficiently; the error rate and the number of wrong decisions rise. In addition, further operational implications become apparent: colleagues of workaholics hand in their notice or become ill, and the motivation and productivity within the team decline. A general feeling of uncertainty and helplessness develops within the company about what is happening and how to react to it. If they let the process run its course, it will end in an absolute crisis in Phase 3: The workaholics will continue to work neither effectively nor efficiently; the number of mistakes will increase, and those affected will drop out due to severe illness, sometimes for the long term. On top of the increasing staff fluctuation,

1 For the purpose of readability, the male form will be used to represent both the male and female in this study.

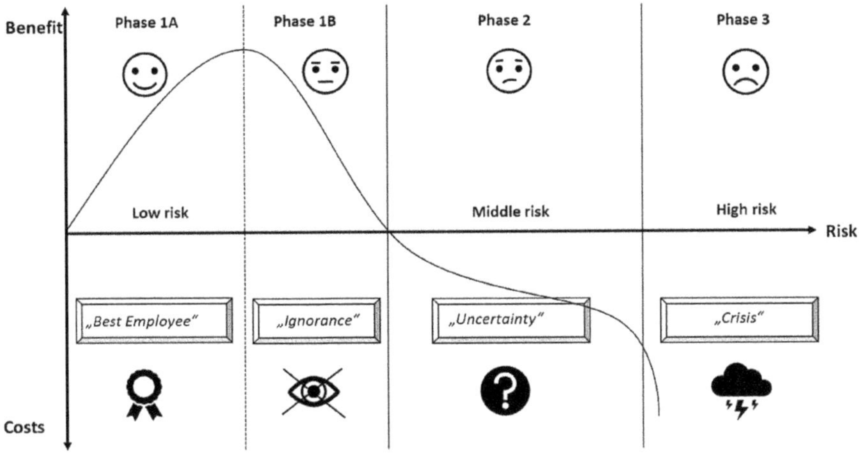

Figure 1: Cost-Benefit-Graph Workaholism
(Source: Own illustration)

the increased absences as well as the declining motivation, further significant economic losses may occur: failure to conclude contracts, customers walking away, important projects stagnating. When this point is reached, the company may find itself in a situation that existentially threatens their economic situation as well as their substance, and in which it will become increasingly difficult to heal the problems created.

The trajectory in Figure 1 clearly shows the risk potential workaholics pose for companies. The later the employer reacts to the workaholic behaviour, the higher is the risk and the probability of severe economic damages occurring.

The objectives of the previous examination were firstly to point out potential economic and specifically human resources risks associated with workaholic employees for individual businesses. Secondly the objectives were to conduct an empirical analysis of the presence of indications for workaholism (symptoms, characteristics and types of workaholism) in companies. Thirdly the objectives were to point out how operational frameworks trigger or promote workaholism.

The target group of the study was human resources managers. The aim was to demonstrate that this perspective could deliver sufficient indications to identify workaholic behaviour.

Back then, the study arrived at the essential finding that the human resources sector was generally aware of workaholism, but it was taken seriously neither by human resources managers nor by society.

It can be stated that the increasing public awareness of the workaholism issue has, to this day, not led the human resources sector to actively and comprehensively address the issue within companies. For this reason, the current empirical study has been developed to illustrate in depth, what effect the workaholic behavioural patterns of employees can have on the economic and human resources situation of a company. Moreover, it will outline which human resources risks hide behind workaholic behaviours and how businesses can actively work to identify workaholism and to address it within the framework of their duty of care towards the affected employees as well as towards their economic interests and their responsibility towards their shareholders.

The more in-depth examination of the topic deliberately asks questions parallel to the 2005 study, to ensure a direct comparability between the results of the first study and the current results. The fundamental change was the new test subject target group. The current questionnaire, for the first time in a study in a German speaking country, asked those afflicted with workaholism themselves about their behavioural traits and their effects on business. The identifier workaholism manifested itself in the active participation of Workaholics Anonymous groups in Germany, Austria and Switzerland.

In Chapter 2,[2] the theoretical background in regard to workaholism is introduced. This is followed by a description of types of workaholism from a therapeutic, advisory and psychological perspective and a discussion on which types are to be the focus of the investigation. The characteristics and symptoms of the addiction, as well as its progression, are used to illustrate the extent of the addiction.

Subsequently, the background of human resources risk management is outlined. A workaholic employee also, as explained earlier, has a negative impact on operational processes and carries economic and human resources risks for the company. The fundamentals of operational risk management are outlined as a theoretical basis for Chapters 4 and 5, which in this study, for the second time in workaholism research, puts the focus on human resources risks in general and specifically in relation to workaholism. It consults the risk areas' bottleneck risk, resignation risk, adjustment risk and motivation risk according to Kobi (see Kobi 2002 a, p. 35 ff.), to qualitatively discuss the risk potential of the different types of workaholism with regard to economic and human resources ramifications.

---

2 In Chapters 2 – 3 the theoretical principles that form the basis for the empirical survey are outlined. As this is a comparative study, these principles have been, in principal, taken from the 2005 publication/study and updated.

It does this by giving examples of the consequences for co-workers and for the workaholic himself. The economic approach puts the focus on the potential loss of added value for the company, and the human resources perspective makes the connection to the human being and illustrates concrete human resources ramifications, such as the renewed recruitment process caused by a resignation.

The theoretical insights introduced in Chapters 2 and 3 are empirically examined and discussed in Chapter 4. An explorative empirical study in the form of a standardised questionnaire has been carried out, which dealt with indicators of workaholism, exerting operational influences with the ability to cause or promote workaholism, as well as the effects on a company from the point of view of workaholics.

In Chapter 5 follows an extensive risk analysis on the basis of the survey results with respect to workaholic behavioural characteristics, symptoms of workaholism and operational influences on the development or promotion of workaholism.

Finally, Chapter 6 introduces instruments for a risk analysis of workaholism in companies and provides recommendations for actions facilitating a pragmatic implementation. It also discusses the specific role and responsibility of management in relation to the workaholic employee, and outlines instruments management can use to identify workaholic behavioural traits.

2 Theoretical background of workaholism

This chapter introduces the theoretical background of workaholism. More specifically, it introduces possible types of workaholism from a therapeutic, advisory and psychological perspective and a discussion on which types are to be the focus of the investigation. Following that, it illustrates the characteristics and symptoms of the addiction as well as the progression of the addiction.[3]

2.1 Differentiation between addiction and workaholism

The term 'addiction' is generally associated with the addiction to substances such as alcohol, drugs or pills, while the term as such has not established itself in the international classification of psychological disorders, ICD-10 of the World Health Organisation (WHO) and the Diagnostic and Statistical Manual of Mental Disorders V. Version (DSM-V), of the American Psychiatric Association.

It can be said that addiction takes on a compensatory value for a perceived deficiency or grievance, which can be traced back to a developmental disorder originating in early childhood. It is also apparent that addiction not dependent on substances (= substance-free) still plays no significant role in medically and psychological addiction research to date. Only gambling addiction gets a mention under the category of 'Personality and Behavioural Disorders' in the ICD-10-GM, in terms of abnormal habits and impulse control disorders, and is recognised as a condition by health insurers. But also here, the term 'addiction' is not used, but rather that of 'pathological gambling'.[4] However, psychologists in their therapeutic practice are increasingly confronted with the phenomenon of substance-free addiction (see Gross 1990, p. 9, Berger 2014, p. 1). Against this background, Wilson-Schaef/Fassel define addiction as '…each substance or each process, ruling our life and towards which we are powerless.' (Wilson-Schaef/Fassel 1994, p. 58). Addiction becomes apparent if a person is controlled by the two main categories of addiction, substance addiction or process addiction, and if this leads to compulsive behaviour. In substance addiction, substances are

3 More in-depth information on the topics features in Chapter 2 of Meißner 2005.
4 ICD-10-GM Version 2017, Chapter V Psychological and Behavioural Disorders, F63.0. ICD-10-GM is the international statistical classification of illnesses and related health issues, 10th Revision, German Modification. It is the official classification for the encoding of diagnoses in outpatient and inpatient care in Germany. (https://www.dimdi.de/static/de/klassi/icd-10-gm/index.htm).

introduced to the body, leading to a physical dependence, such as alcohol, drugs, cigarettes or food. Process addiction, however, relates to activities or interactions which influence a person in such a way that he may become addicted to them and may no longer be able to rationally control himself. Examples of process addictions are gambling, relationship, sex, and internet addiction as well as compulsive buying and workaholism (Wilson-Schaef/Fassel 1994, p. 58 ff., see Niebling 1997, p. 21). In substance-free addictions, the body is able, by external stimuli alone '...to create a biochemical situation, enabling an addiction-like[5] experience, addiction without drugs as it were.' (Gross 1990, p. 12). In numerous interviews with workaholics, Wilson-Schaef and Fassel determined that the 'fix' does not necessarily lie within the work itself, but in the adrenaline rush that comes with the work. The rush makes them feel alive and full of energy (see Wilson-Schaef/Fassel 1994, p. 121). On a critical note, one might add that the above definition and description suggest that the drug or the action itself is elevated to the subject of the process and impacts on the person of its own accord. In truth, however, the person himself is the initiator of the start of the addiction, because it is he who decides to take the drug and he himself carries the responsibility for it (see Büchner 1993, p. 152). The addiction is the 'unhealthy' decision for using the drug and its effect on the mental and physical state. This state is reached by consuming the drug, in this case their own working behaviour, whereby it is irrelevant, whether it is a substance or a substance-free addiction (see Gross 1990, p. 15). The fact that the addiction significantly influences a person in his actions is to be seen as a subsequent reaction. The addict succumbs to the fallacy to surrender responsibility for his life to the addiction. Wolf defines workaholism somewhat broader than Wilson-Schaef and Fassel, by also including unpaid work, such as housework, property renovation or volunteer work. 'Workaholism is a dynamically progressing pathological fixation on activity and serves the repression of psychological problems, while the activity or its necessity is used as a defence mechanism against having to deal with one's own feelings.' (Wolf 2002, p. 89). What differentiates workaholism from the other substance-free addictions is not only the dependence on an increased adrenaline level, but also the addiction to the concrete process of work. Herein lies the danger for the addict, who often tends towards overconfidence and continues to work, even when the strength of his body declines (see Fassel 1994, p. 19 f).

5 It is to be noted that Gross, in this context, speaks of 'addiction-like', which constitutes a limitation of the term 'addiction'. The experience of substance addiction must be identical with that of substance unrelated addiction, as it would otherwise not constitute an *addiction*.

When differentiating workaholism from non-addictive working behaviours, the term 'loss of control' is of central significance, which means the degree of ability to make choices and to exercise free will in work behaviour. The addiction is not measured by what the addict does, or how much of it, but by what he is no longer able to do, for example to enjoy leisure or pleasure (see Berger 2002, p. 2). Since loss of control, as well as the observed withdrawal symptoms characteristic of workaholism, also characterise substance addiction, workaholism is considered an illness in this study.[6] A prerequisite of this form of addiction is the availability of the addictive drug 'work'. The available literature documents workaholism primarily among those in gainful employment. This group comprises managers and politicians, whose reputation, power and income are dependent on their 'tireless' application to work, artists, poets, writers or other self-employed individuals, such as doctors, lawyers, craftsmen, for whom reputation and income are pivotal, priests, teachers, hospital staff, social workers, 'helping' professions, for whom the confirmation of their self-image also plays a significant role.[7] Please note, not everybody who works a lot and works hard is a workaholic. There are numerous

6 The diagnostic criteria for addiction to psychotropic substances are described in ICD-10-GM 2017, F 00, amongst others, through the following criteria: 1. Acute intoxication after consumption of psychotropic substance. 2. Consumption of the substance leads to damaged health (for example depression). 3. Dependency syndrome: Typically, there is a strong urge to consume the substance. The affected person finds it difficult to control the consumption. He continues to use the substance, despite damaging consequences. The substance use has priority over other activities and obligations. The tolerance level increases over time and sometimes there is the physical withdrawal syndrome. 4. Amnestic syndrome, which goes along with memory impairment, a disruption of time perception and the time grid become apparent. (https://www.dimdi.de/static/de/klassi/icd-10-gm/kodesuche/onlinefassungen/htmlgm2017/block-f10-f19.htm) If one compares these criteria with the types of workaholism (Section 2.2.), the characteristics of workaholism (Section 2.3.) as well as the symptoms of workaholism (Section 2.4.), there is a striking similarity between substance addiction and workaholism, which reinforces the view of workaholism as an illness.

7 There are further types of workaholism, occurring independent of gainful employment. Dependent employees, who have little decision-making authority at their work, have a monotonous job, or are always working under instruction, may perceive their work as unsatisfactory, as they, for example, receive only little recognition or confirmation. They may compensate this frustration with work, by compulsory seeking secondary employment or volunteer positions or offer excessive neighbourhood support. Also, those not in gainful employment such as housewives may develop workaholism, which may manifest, for example, in compulsory cleaning or excessive care (see Heide 2000, p. 6 f.). What they all have in common is that they are addicted to the adrenaline rush that comes with work.

reasons to work beyond the normal measure for a time. Schwochow poses the decisive question here: 'Does the hard-working individual still have his work under control or is the work in control of the hard-working individual?' (Schwochow 1997, p. 42). As long as the work is not associated with self-abandonment through relentless activity, i.e. the 'hard-working individual' is still able to relax in his leisure time and can devote time to his private life, without thinking of work, there is no addictive behaviour present (see Oellerking 2002, p. 272).

As this study focusses on how the human resources sector deals with the issue of workaholism, the determining factor for the definition is that workaholism is to be regarded as a process addiction, referring to remunerated activity, meaning gainful employment. In relation to addiction theory, workaholism, in this study, is understood as follows:

Workaholism is an internal compulsive and pathological fixation on work (gainful employment), on work results or on working in the sense of activity, where the addict surrenders or sacrifices himself to one or all of these aspects. The addict surrenders the responsibility for his own actions in relation to himself and in relation to his environment, and thereby loses control over them.

Workaholics do not necessarily experience work as a purposive and productive activity, but rather as a means to an end, to be able to live out the addiction.

2.2 Types of workaholism

This work relates to the types of workaholism Robinson and Fassel have identified over the many years of their therapeutic and advisory work. The practical examples the experts attribute to workaholism represent professionally grounded external assessments, which seem plausible for the description of a corporate reality.

Robinson is a family therapist, who undertook the clustering of types of workaholism on the basis of various case histories from his own practice. The types as described by Fassel result from her long-standing experience as a business consultant, in which she encountered a large number of workaholics.

2.2.1 Types according to Robinson

a) The relentless workaholic

Most common in society are the relentless workaholics. They constantly and compulsively work day and night, at the weekends and on public holidays. They do not take breaks, are unable to relax, as they compulsively want to keep to their deadlines. They have lost the ability to judge whether a task is complete. To them, work is more important than relationships and other people's feelings. When a job is done, they urgently have to begin another; they are perfectionists, and nobody satisfies their requirements (see Robinson 2014, p. 36 f.).

b) The bulimic workaholic

The bulimic workaholic sways between sudden binges of work mania and lethargy. Their modus operandi is characterised by procrastination and frantic work. The procrastination can be ascribed to the fear of not being up to the task. They feel paralysed and unable to work and feel an inner compulsion not to work. Thus, beginning the task will be delayed for such a period of time that they will slip into a state of panic due to existing expected outcomes and then, under a surge of adrenaline, work frantically and without break. This is followed by a state of physical exhaustion, during which the workaholic collapses, sleeps for several days and nights in a row and sometimes is not even able to change his clothes. This behaviour is equal to that of an alcoholic, sleeping off his intoxication. After such a work binge or episode follows a phase of 'normality', during which he does not work excessively, and an outsider will not notice anything unusual (see Robinson 2014, p. 38 f.).

c) The attention-deficit workaholic

The attention-deficit workaholic subconsciously seeks excitement, crises and strong stimuli. They constantly live on the edge of chaos. They find it hard to concentrate on a task. They get bored quickly and fling themselves head over heels into the next project, without having completed the old one, just to get a new surge of adrenalin. Details, thorough research and preparation are of no interest to them; they feel euphoria, when they are trying out new ideas and are able to begin several projects simultaneously. They often do not take the opinion of others into account. They find it hard to finalise a matter. The consequences may be catastrophic, when the addiction ultimately prohibits careful planning (see Robinson 2014, p. 39 f.).

d) The savouring workaholic

The modus operandi of the savouring workaholic is slow, deliberate and methodical. Their perfectionism forces them to live in a permanent state of insecurity that a task, that is finished in principle, is not good enough, and has to be permanently reworked. They find it very hard to evaluate when a task is done, which often leads to them not being able to adhere to deadlines. Individual work steps are recorded in detailed lists, which may take longer than the actual task. The workaholic 'savours' the work like an alcoholic 'savours a drink'. This work method makes it hard for them to work in a team, as they often face the criticism that they are holding up the work of the group. When the group is ready to move on to the next point, savouring workaholics are still analysing the previous one, examining it from various perspectives and wanting to revise the plans again. They find it hard to finalise projects and begin new ones, even if their colleagues see it differently (see Robinson 2014, p. 41 f.).

e) The caring workaholic

The caring workaholic feels the constant urge to take responsibility for other people, to empathise with them and to always be there for them. In the process, they forget to care for themselves and work day and night for others. The justification for this behaviour is governed by noble motives and can mainly be found in the helping professions such as nurses or clerics. They are happy when they are helping others, as this gives them the feeling that they are needed. If they can look after the problems and feelings of others, they think, feel and act, as if they were almighty. This sense of duty becomes an excessive burden on them; they put pressure on themselves and exhaust their physical energy (see Robinson 2000, p. 70 f.).

2.2.2 Types according to Fassel

a) The compulsive worker

Compulsive workers are constantly driven towards work and show the following characteristics:

- They are the first to arrive at work and the last to leave
- They take work on holiday with them, if they even go on holiday
- They also work, when nobody expects them to do so and there is no prescribed deadline
- They are perfectionists and work thoroughly
- They are insincere, keep their work projects secret from others and build up a 'work stash'
- They have a narrowed view and justify their work compulsion by making the point that they are only working to secure a high standard of living for their family (see Fassel 1990, p. 17 f.)

b) The binge worker

This addiction type has the same characteristics as the compulsive worker. The distinguishing criterion is in the intensity of the manifestation. They seemingly act normal, until they launch into a fit of working frantically, equivalent to an alcoholic or compulsive eater launching into a drinking or eating frenzy. During such an episode of work mania they sometimes do not sleep for several nights and have lost all perception of time. This obsession leads to a numbing of all other areas of their own lives. After an episode, they feel drained, comparable to an alcoholic with a 'hangover' (see Fassel 1990, p. 18 f.)

c) The closet worker

In comparison to the compulsive worker, who also keeps his work processes secret, the closet workaholic has previously been exposed publicly and, as a reaction, now hides his work from others. He consequently works in secret, when the probability of being found out is very low. He finds excuses, for example, on holiday, to not do something together with his partner, and to work during this time instead. Another form of clandestine working is the generous definition of what constitutes *one* task in need of completing. This is communicated, and it is promised that he will pursue only this one task and then work no more. But in reality, this task is subdivided into many sub-tasks which all need completing, so that it is only one task for appearance's sake, and the partner is being lied to, so that the workaholic can pursue the addiction (see Fassel 1990, p. 20 f.).

d) The work anorexic

Work avoidance is a main criterion of this type. They are driven by the urge to avoid work, as they are convinced they are not allowed to make mistakes. This is the reason tasks are not even begun or are delayed. The delaying causes feelings of guilt, which render the addict unable to act, which lead them to avoid contact with other people. Often, these addicts suffer from a lack of self-awareness. They do not know where their limits are and when they have done enough work. Work is, therefore, completed under immense pressure and is only half finished. The dilemma of this form of addiction is that the addicts are trapped in a constant rush and that they stop asking themselves whether this is what they really want and what the benefit is to them. The gain is on the outside only: They receive something, by losing themselves (see Fassel 1990, p. 23 f.).

This puts the study on a foundation clearly describing the reality, especially since there are clear parallels in the classification of types. Both describe the worker suffering from work episodes and Fassel's compulsive worker is comparable to Robinson's relentless workaholic.

Given that, the following types of workaholism will form the basis of this study, as their behavioural patterns are clearly identifiable from a company's point of view:

- The compulsive/relentless workaholic
- The binge/bulimic workaholic

- The attention-deficit workaholic
- The savouring workaholic

Fassel's closet worker is excluded, as this distinctive feature can rather be found in a private environment. The type of the caring workaholic will also be excluded from the presentation, as it mainly occurs in the 'helping' professions, which are not the focus of this study. The work anorexic will also be excluded.

2.3 Characteristics of workaholism

The characteristics of substance-free addictions are comparable to those of substance addiction. Already in 1979, Mentzel found, when examining his patients, that the behaviour of workaholics equalled that of alcoholics (see Mentzel 1979, p. 115). From this, he and therapists respectively counsellors, such as Robinson, Wilson-Schaef or Fassel arrived at the conclusion to refer to it as work *addiction* (workaholism) and to regard it as an illness. In the following, there will be outlined various characteristics of workaholism, which will aid in the identification of workaholics and give clues on how to identify the respective type of workaholism.

- *Workaholics are always very busy and are always in a hurry.* It is striking that they use every minute and accept permanent delays (see Robinson 2000, p. 58, see Robinson 2014, p. 32).
- *They want to have everything under control.* They regard delegating tasks or a request for help as a sign of weakness or incompetence. Work is minutely organised and planned with perfectionism, so everything is controllable. Spontaneity and flexibility are being hampered in the process (see Robinson 2000, p. 58, see Robinson 2014, p 32, see Fassel 1990, p. 39 f).
- *Nothing is ever good enough for them.* They have a perfectionist expectation of themselves, i.e. they always have an answer, always have a solution ready and make no mistakes. Driven by the obsession of not being good enough, of not doing enough and not managing, they define a standard for themselves, which they also use to evaluate the performance of others, who can never fulfil these impossible expectations (see Robinson 2000, p. 58; see Robinson 2014, p 32, see Wilson-Schaef/Fassel 1994, p. 64, see Heide 1999, p. 4, see Fassel 1990, p. 40).
- *Their relationships suffer under their work.* Their mind often remains at work and they neglect private relationships. Family celebrations, birthdays or holidays are forgotten, ignored or deemed unimportant (see Robinson 2000, p. 59, see Robinson 2014, p 32, see Fassel 1990, p 42).[8]

8 See Footnote 6, Comparison with the addiction to psychotropic substances.

- *They have work binges.* Deadlines are set in such a way that they can only be adhered to in an 'intoxicated' state of work. During this 'intoxication' they forget themselves. Then, they often smoke a lot, eat little and do not sleep at all, until the work is done, and the addict is physically exhausted and wakes up from the intoxication. This state is comparable with an alcoholic waking up after a drinkingbinge (see Robinson 2000, p. 61, see Robinson 2014, p 33).[9]
- *They are nervous and grumpy.* If they are not working, they will develop a negative conscience. When dealing with friends, they will become nervous and grumpy, as they perceive leisure time as wasted time (see Robinson 2000, p. 59, see Robinson 2014, p 33).
- *They work themselves into a trance.* This state can be compared to the 'blackouts' an alcoholic may experience: After long conversations, they are not able to remember everything, they make serious mistakes when driving, often causing accidents (see Robinson 2000, p. 60, see Robinson 2014, p 33).[10]
- *They are impatient.* Impatience may lead to impulsive reactions, as they have not taken the time for intensive research work preparation. This will lead to preventable mistakes (see Robinson 2000, p. 60, see Robinson 2014, p 33).
- *They believe they are only as good as their last success.* As soon as a work task is completed, they feel empty, restless and depressed. Their wellbeing often only returns with a new task (see Robinson 2000, p. 61, see Robinson 2014, p. 35).
- *They have no time for themselves.* They sacrifice their entire time for their work. Healthy eating, rest and exercise are neglected or practised in excess. There are workaholics who eat healthily and exercise to a strict programme, to preserve their health for even harder work. This enables them to extend their addiction even further (see Wilson-Schaef/Fassel 1994, p. 121 f.). Even, when physical complaints arise (headache, high blood pressure, ulcers), workaholics have no time to go to the doctor (see Robinson 2000, p. 61, see Robinson 2014, p 35). People who are primarily addicted to work, additionally often suffer from secondary addictions, happening in the background. Usually, this manifests in heavy smoking or coffee drinking, in relationship addictions or compulsive eating. They overwork themselves and are trying to uphold their concentration with cigarettes and coffee, with replenishing themselves by eating too much, or staying at the office longer, which in turn leads to relationship or family problems (see Fassel 1990, p. 28, see Fassel 1994, p. 47, see Mentzel 1979, p. 134). The adrenaline rush of excessive working can be so high that

---

9 See Footnote 6, Comparison with the addiction to psychotropic substances

10 See Footnote 6, Comparison with the addiction to psychotropic substances.

the addict is unable to relax, even if he wanted to. (see Fassel 1990, p. 34, see Fassel 1994, p. 53 ff.).

- *Denial and insincerity.* Denial is the main defence mechanism and the primary defence strategy in the addiction progression. It is characteristic of workaholism that this denial does not appear as such, as this form of addiction is met with positive recognition by the public. Workaholics deny their addiction in different dimensions. Some draw comparisons ('Workaholism is still better than…'), others bargain ('Workaholism is good, because through it I have achieved such and such great things') or others admit to workaholism and believe it is not dangerous. The latter form of denial carries the danger of impaired judgement and the reduced ability to make decisions, which will become stronger and stronger with the progression of the addiction and a risk to all involved (see Fassel 1990, p. 29 f, see Fassel 1994, p. 47 f.). Hand in hand with this, goes the insincerity of addicts trying to keep up the façade to the outside world. They lie to themselves to avoid coming into touch with their own feelings and needs. They also lie to the people in their direct environment, to be able to pursue their addiction, and they lie to society, to keep up appearances (see Wilson-Schaef/Fassel 1994, p. 63 f.) The insincerity is often based in the addicts' inability to self-evaluate. They tend to over or underestimate themselves, as they find it hard to accept themselves. They exaggerate strongly, when portraying their performance, and mistakes are seldom mentioned (see Fassel 1990, p. 30 f, see Fassel 1994, p. 49, see Heide 1999, p. 4).
- *External referenting.* Workaholics strongly orient themselves towards the outside world, to direct their behaviour accordingly and to do what is seemingly expected, to secure their own survival. This behaviour, for example, includes the meticulous keeping of lists, which serve as the irrevocable framework of their lives. Whatever is not on the list, will not get done. With workaholics, these lists go so far that they also contain private appointments such as playing with the kids. If this point is not listed, the children are not played with (see Fassel 1990, p. 32 f, see Fassel 1994, p. 50 f.).
- *Compulsion.* The compulsion of workaholism expresses itself in the addict being constantly driven by work and thus he effectively has lost control over his actions, which he would never admit. To hold on to the supposed control over their actions, they work out sophisticated time management systems and task lists and build up 'a stash' of work, to avoid creating the feeling that there is nothing left to be done (see Fassel 1990, p. 36 f, see Fassel 1994, p. 55 ff.).[11]

11 See Footnote 6, comparison with the addiction to psychotropic substances.

Table 1: Allocation of addiction characteristics to types of workaholism

● = highly pronounced ○ = pronounced	Compulsive/relentless workaholic	Binge/bulimic workaholic	Attention-deficit workaholic	Savouring workaholic	Work anorexic
Workaholics are always very busy and are always in a hurry	●		○		
They want to have everything under control	●	○			
Nothing is ever good enough for them	●	●		●	●
Their relationships suffer under their work	●	●	○	○	○
They have work binges	○	●			
They are nervous and grumpy	●	○	○		
They work themselves into a trance	○	●			
They are impatient	●	○	●		○
They believe, they are only as good as their last success	●		○	○	○
They have no time for themselves	●	○	○	○	●
Denial and insincerity	●	●	●	●	●
External orientation	●	●			
Compulsion	●	●	●	●	●

(Source: Meißner 2005, p. 48: Own illustration)

Table 1 carries out a rough allocation of the characteristics of the respective types of workaholism, which are to be seen as a guide.

2.4 Symptoms, phases and progression of the addiction

Symptoms of addiction seen in workaholics may be physical and behavioural. These are summed up in Table 2 and provide a comprehensive description.

Table 2: Physical and behavioural symptoms of workaholism

Externally visible physical symptoms	Externally invisible physical symptoms
• Allergies • Shortness of breath (high blood pressure) • Nervous tics • Dizziness • Trembling hands	• Headache • Permanent exhaustion • Digestive problems • Stomach pain • Ulceration • Stinging in the chest (heart disease) • Back pain • Sudden hearing loss

Externally visible behavioural symptoms	Externally invisible behavioural symptoms
• Mood swings (euphoria / depression, mental illnesses) • Concentration problems • Outbursts of anger • Unrest • Forgetfulness • Hyperactivity • Irritability and impatience	• Tension • Sleep disorders • Inability to relax • Boredom

(Source: Meißner 2005, p. 49: Own compilation following Robinson 2000, p. 61; Fassel 1994, p. 65 f., Mentzel 1979, p. 134 f.)[12]

The correspondence of characteristics of workaholism to those of substance addiction, deduced from individual therapeutic cases, are also evident in the progression of the addiction. Also, workaholism is a dynamic process, going through different stages and might ultimately end in death as the highest stage of escalation.

The established literature on stages and progression of addiction basically orients itself along the stages of workaholism, which Fassel has defined as follows and which are detailed in Table 3:[13]

12 See Footnote 6, comparison with the addiction to psychotropic substances.

13 The scale resembles the Jellnick scale, which was originally used for the diagnosis and treatment of alcoholism.

Table 3: Stages of Workaholism

Stage	Symptoms	
Early Stage	• Feeling of efficiency, of the strain of action and of self-determination • Rushing, busyness, worry and helper syndrome • Inability to say "No" • Constant thinking about the work • Secret work	• Obsession to set up lists • Overestimation of own abilities • No free days • Constantly more than forty weeks of work
Middle Stage	• Other addictions increase: food, alcohol, smoking, buying, sex / love • Social life is shrinking and does not exist • Neglect of relationships and related obligations • Attempts to change the behaviour will fail • Physical exhaustion, sleep problems, headache and back pain • Phases of apathy	
Final Stage	• Chronic headache / back pain, high blood pressure, stomach ulcer, depression • Brain stroke or heart attack, severe illness, hospitalisation, severe mental illness • Blackouts at work or in traffic, airholes "stare" • Emotionally dead • Moral and spiritual bankruptcy • Death	

(Source: Meißner 2005, p. 50: following Fassel 1994, p. 71; Gross 1990, p. 119; Heide 2000, p. 4)

In the early stage, work is characterised by a feeling of performance and wanting to prove oneself. A good performance is rewarded with even more responsible tasks and, due to the high societal status of work, a narrowing of personal interest towards the addictive drug work creeps in. The work approach is characterised by rushing, busyness, overcaring and 'rescuing' others. Addicts' own families are neglected more and more, as the addicts permanently take on new tasks and do not say 'No' any more, whereby the addicts often impose more on themselves than they can handle. This leads to the addicts constantly thinking of work and them experiencing a fear of failure. To reach their quota, they draw up detailed lists, extend their daily working hours, also work at the weekend, keep their work secret from others, begin to lie or deceive themselves, and little by little lose control over themselves, as they no longer sense their physical and psychological boundaries (see Fassel 1990. p. 47 f, see Fassel 1994, p. 69 f., see Heide 2000, p. 4). In the middle stage, the workaholics realise that their life is run by something else and they begin to defend their illness or deny it, by increasingly lying. To manage their workload, other addictions in aid of maintaining their performance levels come into play, such as eating or alcohol addiction, heavy smoking or coffee consumption. Social relationships are strongly neglected at this stage, as the addict's time is taken up by work, and he fears that those close to him may address his problematic behaviour. Phases of physical exhaustion and phases of apathy increase; the permanent adrenaline rushes may lead to sleeping problems. Even if the addict tries to change during this stage, this attempt is destined to fail, as he is in denial about his illness, and merely seeks short term recovery. There is an increased occurrence of illnesses such as headaches or backaches (see Fassel 1990, p. 50 f, see Fassel 1994, p. 73 f., see Heide 2000, p. 4). In the final stage, workaholics display schizophrenic behavioural patterns, which alternate between times of intensive activity and apathy. The danger of blackouts during work or while behind the wheel of a car increases; sometimes the addict has no memory of certain activities or periods of time. The illnesses are becoming so severe in this phase that they seriously impair the workaholic. There is a strong increase, especially in chronic headaches and back pain, high blood pressure, stomach ulcers and depression, forcing the workaholic to rest. If these signals are ignored, the illnesses progress and may lead to a heart attack or stroke, or long hospital stays. The workaholic registers his illness; he feels emotionally dead and spiritually bankrupt. If he does not manage to handle his addiction at this stage, it may well end in death (see Fassel 1990, p 52, see Fassel 1994, p. 74 f.).

Table 4 allocates, in summary, the secondary illnesses occurring with workaholism at the different stages, noting that the boundaries are fluid.

Table 4: Symptoms and stages of workaholism

Stages	**Characteristics/Consequences**
1. Early stage	Nervous tics
	Outbursts of anger
	Unrest
	Forgetfulness
	Hyperactivity
	Irritability and impatience
	Digestive problems
	Stomach pain
	Tension
	Colds and 'flu'
2. Middle stage	Allergies
	Concentration problems
	Headaches
	State of permanent exhaustion
	Back pain
	Acute hearing loss/tinnitus
	Sleep disorders, unable to relax
3. Final stage	High blood pressure (shortness of breath)
	Dizziness
	Stomach ulcers
	Mood swings, depression, severe mental illnesses
	Chest pain (heart disease)

(Source: Own illustration)

This shows that in the early stage, the symptoms visible to the outside are generally inconspicuous and do not yet necessarily require medical treatment. Only in the middle stage do illnesses requiring medical treatment increase and, thus, become visible not only for third parties and family members, but also for medical professionals.

3 Human resources risk management in regard to workaholism

Economic business interests make it a core task of companies to identify potential risks and develop counter measures, to stave off or minimise a loss in value. The necessary examination of human resources risks in this context has only rudimentary representation in classic risk management systems. The importance of the maintenance and development of the human capital employed for the achievement of corporate success is underestimated.

Risks have to be defined, recorded, continuously evaluated and monitored through control mechanisms as part of the risk management. 'Risk management is identified as the totality of all measures, with which the dangers of a reduction in success are to be identified, lessened and the occurrence of damages prevented or their consequences mitigated.' (Hochrein 1999, p. 20). It is the task of management to define the company's risk strategy and establish a functioning risk management system (see Gerke 2003, p. 26, see Lück 1998, p. 8). An effective risk management requires an advanced risk awareness among the employees as well as a respective company-specific risk culture (see Hochrein 1999, p. 13 f.). Risk is understood as '... the potential danger of losses from business activity, i.e. the negative deviation of the business development from the planned values, caused by a general uncertainty of future results, in combination with an incomplete level of information.' (see Bitz 2000, p. 13).

As risks endanger company objectives, they correspond directly to them. In the identification and evaluation of risks, the risks working on the company from its surroundings as well as those anchored in operational processes have to be taken into account (see Hochrein 1999, p. 26). According to Füser, these risks may be presented as a risk matrix (see Figure 2). The possible level of risk/damage (quality dimension) and probability of occurrence (intensity dimension) are ranked in accordance with their manifestation (see Füser 1999, p. 753).

The objective of the evaluation of risk management is the reduction of business risk to an adequate level. According to Hochrein and Gerke this is achieved through:

- Risk avoidance, by refraining from entering into risky business activity (for example in warring countries).

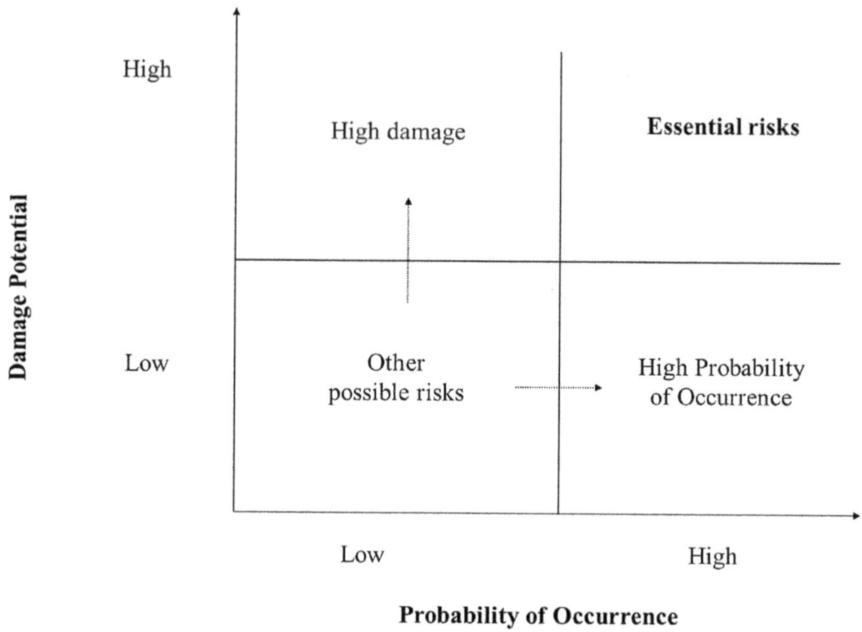

Figure 2: Risk matrix
(Source: see Hochrein 1999, p. 28., Füser 1999, p. 753)

- Risk reduction or minimisation through measures meant to lower the expected loss value. This affects active measures of risk management, which also implies workaholism risks.
- Transferring risks to third parties (for example suppliers, taking up insurance).
- Risk compensation (for example through offsetting transactions).
- Risk acceptance (for example through reserve funds) (see Hochrein 1999, p. 30, see Gerke 2003, p. 26).

Workaholic behaviour in a human resources sense constitutes a deviation from the expected optimum behaviour of the 'normal' employee, which may have a negative effect on the business. Robinson quotes a study on workaholics, from which knowledge was gained on the optimal worker compared to a workaholic, as contrasted in Table 5:

Table 5: Optimal worker versus workaholic

Optimal Workers are:	Workaholics are:
• Good collaborators or delegators	• Unable to delegate work or work as a team
• Interested in the process and outcome	• Only interested in the work itself
• Motivated by intrinsic needs and creative contributions	• Motivated by fear and loss of status
• Efficient, because they see the whole picture as well as the details	• Inefficient because they get bogged down with details
• Creative and risk takers	• No risk takers and not creative
• Able to learn from mistakes	• Unable to tolerate mistakes, they try to avoid them or cover them up

(Source: Meißner 2005, p. 84: Robinson 2014, p. 142 f., without listing Dr Garfield's study as a source)

The Head of the study, Dr Garfield, concluded from the survey, in which 1500 employees from various fields took part, that workaholics do not achieve those top performance levels, they are often assumed to achieve, but that they cause damage to their company, because they are addicted to the work without any interest in the outcome. They are motivated by fear not creativity (see Robinson 2000, p. 203, see Robinson 2014, p. 142 f.). The operational ramifications of workaholism can be manifold throughout the work process, dependent on the type of workaholism.

The risks arising through workaholism are human resources risks, which may prove a threat to the existence of the company, given a certain company size or the number of workaholic employees, or may imply and cause a high loss of value.

3.1 Definition of human resources risks

KonTraG and Basel III[14] give the management of human resources risks a new meaning. The knowledge and the level of motivation of employees are key success factors for service and commercial enterprises.

14 Law on corporate control and transparency (KonTraG) as well as the new capital adequacy requirements for banks (Basel III).

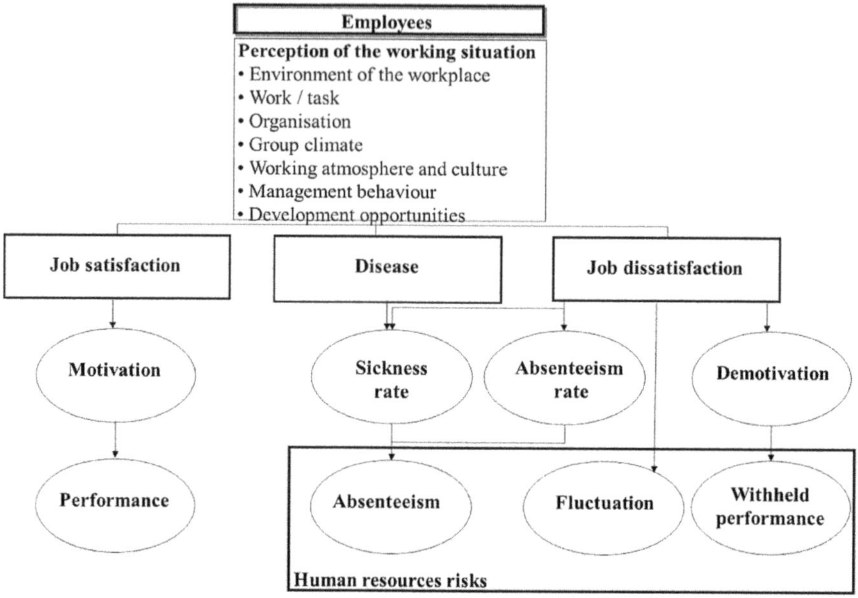

Figure 3: Overview of areas of human resources risks
(Source: Meißner 2005, p. 95: Own compilation following Nieder 1999, p. 142)

Figure 3 elucidates the correlation between employee and work situation and presents the risk areas.[15]

'To address human resources risks means (…) to ask, which employees you will need in future, how to attract them or retain them and how to motivate them to show above average commitment. The aim is to make risks visible and predictable, so that they can be approached preventatively, be limited or avoided.' (Kobi 2002, p. 21) The measurability of human resources risks, according to Kobi, requires a systematic identification, measuring and controlling of human resources risks. He sorts the greatest risks into four areas, restricted to human resources risks, directly caused by employees: bottleneck risk, resignation risk, adjustment risk und motivation risk (see Kobi 2002, p. 21 f.). Ackermann has a broader definition of the term human resources risk, by also subsuming risks, that exist for the personnel, such as workplace and industrial accidents, handling

15 More in-depth information on the topic of Chapter 3 can be found in Meißner 2005.

hazardous materials, specifically environmental stress caused by dust, noise, adverse light conditions, heat, cold, or a lack of ergonomically optimised workplace design at the office or on the factory floor (see Ackermann 1999, p. 70 f.). In addition, his definition of the term human resources risk comprises those risks arising from personnel management, for example within personnel recruitment or personnel development, as well as those risks arising from the company's environment (see Ackermann 1999, p. 73):

a) Changes to the economic environment on the sales and procurement side

For example, unexpected market development with consequences for the personnel requirements, unexpected tariff changes regarding rising wages and salaries with consequences for the adherence to the personnel cost budget.

b) Technological developments

The introduction of new technologies may result in changes in the requirement profiles and require implementation or qualification measures, with consequences for the personnel requirement planning and the adherence to the personnel cost budget.

c) Changes in societal values

Changes in societal values have an influence on the value attitude of the employees in regard to work and profession, career, or leisure time, with consequences for personnel requirement planning.

d) Changes due to legal and political conditions

Changes in this area, especially in times of political uncertainty, require an ongoing monitoring and adjustment of the risks. Examples are the regulation of bogus self-employment, marginal employment or fixed-term employment (see Hochrein 1999, p. 36).

The use of the term 'human resources risk in a broader sense' according to Ackermann is not expedient to this study, as the risks of workaholism are employee immanent and, therefore, are caused by the person himself. For this reason, the term human resources risk will, in the remainder of this study, be used in its narrower sense following Kobi.

Hereafter, the four risk areas are illustrated:

a) Bottleneck risk

In a bottleneck risk situation, the risk is assessed on the basis of a lack of employees, which cannot, or only with great difficulty, be recruited on the employment market (see Kobi 2002, p. 21). There has to be differentiation between demand gaps affecting entire organisational units or key roles, and potential gaps, which can be traced back to individual people. In the identification of demand gaps, Kobi focusses on the consideration of future key roles,[16] changes in the quantative personnel requirements, changes in the qualitative requirements, an analysis of long-term personnel changes (transfers, resignations, retirement), the securing of management and the further development of the company as well as the safeguarding of the staffing of strategic projects (see Kobi 2002a, p. 35). Due to the current skills shortage in Germany, it seems appropriate at this point to not only focus on key roles, when it comes to bottleneck risks, but to assess all company employees as to a potential bottleneck risk. Beyond Kobi's definition, absences, specifically long-term illnesses, should also be taken into consideration, as the staffing within a company is often planned without any, or with only very limited, personnel reserves, so that neither a vacant work space nor a sick employee can be adequately covered by the remaining personnel.

b) Resignation risk

Sudden resignation of staff, not intended by the company, especially of staff in key roles, poses a human resources risk. Due to a lack of employee satisfaction, insufficient career opportunities, or an unsatisfactory corporate or group climate, the company runs the risk that especially those employees holding a key operational role may resign their post (see Bitz 2000, p. 37). A lack of employee satisfaction may imply excessive demand from superiors. Further reasons are given under motivation risk in connection with 'internal resignation'. The risk potential is increased, when departing key players woo away important employees from the company and, by doing so, increase the knowledge gap accordingly (see Giefer 2003, p. 22).

c) Adjustment risk

Fast technological developments, restructurings, fusion and strategic re-orientation devalue existing knowledge with increasing speed. Tendentially,

16 Key functions are functions/skills, which have a large influence on the success of a company and set complex requirements for the acquisition of the required skills (see Kobi 2002a, p. 36).

simple tasks no longer need doing, while the demand for highly qualified staff increases (see Kobi 2002a, p. 95 ff.). The adjustment risk implies, on the one hand, the wrong qualification of employees and, on the other hand, that employees do not want to or are not able to adapt to the necessary changes within the company (see Kobi 2002, p. 21). From adjustment risks arise subsequent risks pertaining to employee expertise and professional development:

Quality risk in regard to employee expertise

If employees do not have the necessary knowledge to fulfil their tasks, there is the risk that the quality of the work results is not at an optimum.

Professional development risk

The professional development risk evaluates, the extent to which, after a qualification measure, there is a knowledge transfer to the professional practice. Executives and human resources management would have to audit the transformation from professional development content to improved work performance.

d) Motivation risk

Motivation risk is understood as the withholding of performances, which are due to psychological and physical stresses as well as an 'internal resignation' (Kobi 2002, p. 21). Kobi defines 'internal resignation' as '...the deliberate or unconscious abandonment of initiative and commitment of an employee or the silent, mental refusal of dedicated performance.' (Kobi 2002a, p. 117). In a slow process, work performance is reduced to a necessary minimum and action by one's own initiative, is refused as quietly and inconspicuously as possible (see Pitsch 2002, p. 55). The reasons for this behaviour lie with the company, the work environment, with the work itself or with the individual.

Indications for this could be a lack of initiative, hyper-conformist behaviour, conflict avoidance, a lack of critical ability, unambitious goals, not fully applying competences, loss of humour, change towards becoming a yes-man, not taking up professional development opportunities, no interest in career advancement, or no participation in professional discussion (see Kobi 2002a, p. 118, Pitsch 2002, p. 56). The holding back of performance potential may also occur with employees who take up management positions early, are overloaded by them and wear themselves out physically and psychologically to such an extent that they become apathetic and develop physical complaints and depression. Similarly, this applies to ambitious personalities, who work a lot, but are not able to achieve their goals (see Kobi 2002a, p. 119 f.). Motivation risk correlates to quality risk.

If performance potential is held back, the risk increases that the quality of work decreases, and tasks are only completed to a minimal optimum. Health complaints are possible consequences and express themselves in an increased risk of absences. A further indication for a lack of motivation is frequent short periods of illness, the so called 'playing hooky' in the sense of absenteeism. Under the heading 'risks, when employees remain with the company', Ackermann has listed further risks, which slot into the area of motivation risk:

- Employees do not stick to the targets agreed with their superiors
- Employees cause disruption and conflict within the team (workplace bullying)
- Employees show no willingness to respect or adapt to the corporate culture
- Employees cause damage, recklessly or consciously and deliberately, for example to equipment, materials, finished goods or through time delays in the completion of their tasks (non-compliance with delivery times)
- Employees cause loss of trust, for example through theft, embezzlement, secret betrayal, or sabotage (see Ackermann 1999, p. 69f.)

The risk of embezzlement/taking undue advantage is magnified by increasing de-centralisation and outsourcing of roles and processes, as the number of external interfaces rises and with it the number of dependent relationships (see Hochrein 1999, p. 36).

3.2 Further human resources risks

Apart from the four risk areas presented, there are further potential human resources risks, which are caused by employees, but cannot be allocated to Kobi's risk areas:

a) Management risks

Potential management risks are an 'inappropriate management style', a lack of authority, insufficient acceptance among people and decisions, a lack of staff motivation (see Hochrein 1999, p. 36), excessive demands pressed on employees, a lack of information and communication.

b) Risk of making wrong decisions

Due to insufficient communication or information, a lack of knowledge, impaired health, or private problems, there is a risk that people make a wrong decision, which may have, in part, far-reaching consequences for the company.

c) Peer to peer pressure

Peer to peer pressure means that colleagues exert pressure on each other to achieve a group target. Pickshaus describes this behaviour as 'the execution of entrepreneurial ruthlessness among employees up to exclusion and bullying.' (see Pickshaus et al. 2001, p. 17). This behaviour can often be traced back to the operational environment. The potential endangerment of the group leads to the employees themselves dividing people into 'dispensable' and 'indispensable'. This results from the fear of becoming dispensable oneself one day (see Glißmann 1999, p. 6). The performance of the group overall, and that of the affected colleague who is subjected to this pressure, can be strongly impaired by the exclusion. Instead of being concentrated on the task, the work energy will potentially be diverted to unproductive behaviour and will not be of added value to the company. The risk of a slump in or loss of performance delivered by the affected party may also have an effect on absences and the resignation risk.

3.3 Human resources risks associated with workaholism and the effects on business

In this section, by means of the types of workaholism of compulsive/relentless workaholics, the binge/bulimic workaholics, attention-deficit workaholics, the savouring workaholics and the anorexic workaholics, the human resources risks associated with workaholism, and the effects they have on business, are qualitatively analysed using examples of the consequences for colleagues or the group as well as for the performance of the affected person himself. As the criteria for the compulsive/relentless workaholic and the binge/bulimic workaholic are almost identical, with the exception of the sudden episodes, they are analysed together for the purpose of this section.

3.3.1 Risk potential of compulsive/relentless workaholics and binge/bulimic workaholics

As depicted in Sections 2.2. and 2.3., the typical characteristics of these types of workaholism are lacking ability to delegate tasks, the high perfectionist demands from their own work and from the performance of others, impatience, insincerity, unpunctuality, denying the addiction as well as a strong orientation towards the outside world. On top of that, there are mood swings and blackouts after sudden fits of frantic working. This extreme behaviour can have the following effects on the group as well as on the workaholic:

a) Delay of work processes

Since this type permanently and compulsively feels 'driven' by work, he is always in a hurry and finds it hard to stick to deadlines. If the workaholic is a member of a process chain, there is the risk for the recipients of the output down the line that they may not be able to meet potential submission deadlines, which may in turn damage in-house and external client relations. Negative feedback more likely affects the whole group rather than the workaholic alone, and will, therefore, have a negative impact on the group climate. Moreover, there is the risk that the addict will often arrive late for meetings and thus cause a time delay.

b) Not utilising synergy effects

Their perfectionist aspiration makes it hard for this type of workaholic to work in a team. They consider the delegation of tasks as well as asking for help a sign of weakness or incompetence. Working together with a team would mean, for them, not to have everything 'under control' themselves and to share tasks. This may lead to two kinds of consequences. Either, the workaholic tries to isolate himself from the team and avoid working together with colleagues, or he tries to dominate the team and to impose his work method and aspiration on the team members. Under the first scenario, any team immanent synergy effects would probably be lost. The spontaneity and creativity of a team would not be utilised for the optimal completion of tasks, which would result in a risk regarding temporal and qualitative losses for work results. Under the second scenario, the group members would be confronted with the situation of not meeting the performance expectations of the addict. The addict often presents his own solution and exempts himself from making mistakes. Often, he will not accept other suggestions and processes. The colleagues might feel overwhelmed by this, as well as patronised and hampered in their performance ability. This would impede the collaboration and there is a risk that only sub-optimal work results may be achieved.

c) Compensation for mistakes

The impatience of this type of workaholic may lead to impulsive reactions, as he has not taken the time for intensive research for, and preparation of, his work. This may lead to mistakes, which may have to be compensated for by the team, as the workaholic is not able to bring the task to a complete finish. The team will likely be confronted by unreliability, which can strongly hamper the collaboration with the addict. The aspects of compensation for mistakes and unreliability pose a risk, which may have significant economic consequences for a company.

d) Work binges

For this type of workaholism sudden episodes of working frantically are the primary deviation from the compulsive/relentless workaholic. The members of the group might have to adjust in their work organisation to the working episodes of the addict, to work through their own tasks. As the scheduling for the completion of the task is generally set so tightly by the addict that he works himself into a 'work frenzy' and works until he is physically exhausted. This means that a similar way of working my possibly be imposed on the colleagues dependent on him. The strong time pressures and high work intensity well beyond the normal hours of work, with the associated physical strain, carry economic risks regarding an increased error rate in the work results, and wrong decisions as well as an increased risk of work absences due to physical exhaustion of the colleagues and the workaholic himself.

e) Psychological instability

The workaholic believes that he is only as good as his last success. As soon as a task is supposedly complete, he feels empty, restless and depressed. He displays restless and grumpy behaviour and increasingly tends towards outbursts of anger. This conspicuous behaviour carries the risk that it may make it hard for his colleagues to concentrate on their work, as they emotionally deal with the behaviour of the workaholic. It can be assumed that colleagues will be confronted with unpredictable behaviours that may have a strong influence on the reliability with which the work is completed. Further to this, it is feasible that the criteria of denial and insincerity may provoke strong disputes within the group. Denying the addiction, the workaholic often has diminished judgement, as well as a reduced ability for making decisions. He is often insincere towards himself and the team members, by strongly exaggerating when portraying their performance and only very rarely admitting mistakes. Colleagues may feel deceived and irritated by the behaviour of the workaholic. The reaction might show as incomprehension and resentment. The group climate may be disrupted with a negative effect on work quality, as those affected would spend more time thinking about the tense atmosphere than they would do concentrating on the content of their work. In addition, the company has to calculate the risk carried by wrong decisions.

f) External orientation

The orientation of the workaholic towards the external presumably prevents optimal team work, as it confronts colleagues with unpredictable behaviour.

Synergy effects due to different discussion viewpoints and communal development of task strategies are probably frequently undermined, as workaholics communicate third party opinions, to avoid confrontation.

The economic risk regarding the performance of a workaholic has to focus on the quality of the work results as well as on the risk of wrong decisions. A lack of work preparation, tight scheduling with the associated work pressures, as well as psychological instability, pose a high risk for error-ridden work results and wrong decisions within the work process. The perfectionist style of work cannot compensate for the above criteria, as the self-evaluation of the workaholic diverges from the actual style of work. The unpredictability of the workaholic, especially in an advanced stage, poses a high economic risk.

3.3.2 Risk potential in other types of workaholism

a) Anorexic workaholic

The characteristics of this type are the compulsive avoidance of work for fear of mistakes as well as the associated delay of work. This causes the addicts to work under immense pressure, leading to the works often not being completed at all. Due to a lack of self-awareness, their ability to act is strongly impaired. The attitude of work avoidance may be very irritating for the team colleagues involved. It may make the impression that the workaholic is trying to delegate his tasks to his colleagues, or to deliberately delay work. He is deemed lazy. The group is confronted by the fact that they have to, in part, support the addict in the completion of his tasks, or compensate for his mistakes, so as not to endanger the group result. With this type of workaholic, the economic risks lie within an increased investment in human capital through support services and mistake compensation provided by colleagues.

As the anorexic workaholic often works under a lot of pressure, the risks regarding an increased potential for errors and wrong decisions increase for the company.

b) Attention-deficit workaholic

This type provokes crises, starts several tasks or projects at once, without finishing one, and is euphoric about trying out new ideas. His style of work is superficial without sound planning, and the opinions of colleagues are not taken into account.

The economic risks seem to manifest in the unreliability in the completion of tasks. In order not to endanger a common team objective, the colleagues may face a situation in which they have to compensate for the missing research and planning, and correct potential mistakes as well as finish tasks. The performance of the workaholics is not reliably quantifiable or fully usable. Their behaviour is incalculable for the company and, thus, clearly carries an immense potential for economic risk.

c) Savouring workaholic

Due to their perfectionism, these workaholics live in permanent fear that fundamentally completed tasks are not good enough and have to be perpetually revised. Projects are only completed reluctantly, and completion may be delayed.

This type of work behaviour can seriously hamper teamwork. If the group would like to discuss a new point, the addicts may still be analysing the previous one, examining it from different perspectives and wanting to rework plans time and time again. The colleagues likely have to grapple intensively with this behaviour, which increases the risk of time delay and the work result is not qualitatively enhanced. The expected quality of work does not justify the time delay of the process, and implies the risk that deadlines are not adhered to and economic damage occurs (see Robinson 2000, p. 102).

It can be established that economic consequences have to be contemplated with all types of workaholics, varying in the degree of manifestation, whilst the stages of the addiction are not at the forefront of the evaluation. The more advanced the stage, the higher, one may assume, the level of manifestation of the risks. Table 6 shows that the human resources risks connected with the compulsive/relentless workaholic, the binge/bulimic workaholic and the attention-deficit workaholic are significantly higher than those connected to the remaining types. This finding is underpinned by the results of the review of existing literature, which more often than not focuses the occurrence of forms of addictions among the former types.

3.4 Human resources risks associated with workaholism and the effects on human resources

This section will illustrate the human resources risks which are caused by workaholism and which may lead to human resources consequences. Special consideration will be given to the risks involving colleagues and co-workers, as well as risks involving the workaholic himself.

3.4.1 Human resources risks in regard to colleagues and co-workers

The above sections have shown that working together with workaholics implies risks. Even if team members demonstrate fundamental collegiality towards the workaholic and compensate for and tolerate his behaviour initially, the collegial relationship is not sustainably durable. The constellation bears human resources risks, which will be described in the following paragraphs.

a) Resignation and fluctuation risk

In order to remove themselves from the negative environment of a workaholic, there is the risk that colleagues of workaholics will seek a change of role, in-house or externally. The strain on colleagues working together with a compulsive/relentless workaholic and an attention-deficit workaholic is to be regarded as particularly high, especially, if the workaholic is a superior. In the first case, it can be assumed that the high demands and expectations are perceived by the colleagues as psychologically and physically very stressful, particularly as the adjustment to sudden episodes of work frenzy add another factor. In the second case, the unreliability and lack of continuity in the completion of tasks can be primary reasons for an employee to leave the group or their superior's team. If it is about a workaholic superior, a personal change of jobs is, from experience, the last resort for the affected employee, as conversations may lead to the employee being discredited due to a lack of understanding, and he might be pushed into the role of an outsider. For a company, the recruitment process means a costly and time consuming human capital investment.

b) Bottleneck risk

People working together with a workaholic colleague or superior face a higher risk of co-dependency. It has been proven that co-dependent individuals show a similar progression of addictive behaviour as workaholics and also suffer from associated illnesses.

Studies have shown that health complaints as well as regular deadline and performance pressures increase with the number of hours worked per week. If one makes the compulsive/relentless workaholic the focus of our observation, it is logical to assume that the illnesses suffered by co-workers could be in connection with his high performance requirements and his style of work, especially if the superior is a workaholic. One can assume it to be a similar case with the binge/bulimic workaholic. The lack of reliability, and the high intensity of the work in intervals, pose a psychological and physical stress that must not be underestimated, and which is intensified in a dependent relationship. Excessive demand at work, in combination with not enough rest, can lead to a permanent overload, which may find lasting expression in the health complaints discussed above. (see Fergen/Pickshaus 2001, p. 142). To compensate for absences, investment has to be channelled into the recruitment of a replacement, or it means more work for the remaining colleagues. An increased risk of absences in the form of short illnesses also has to be taken into consideration. If an employee suffers from a headache or a light cold, he might ponder whether he is 'sick enough' to stay at home or whether to go to work. If the working relationship is intact, the employees will generally decide in favour of the employer. If the work atmosphere is negatively impacted by the workaholic, a certain risk has to be assumed by experience that the employee will stay at home, to avoid further strain. Health complaints, frequent absences, frustration among employees and fluctuation can, according to Robinson, often be traced back to a workaholic superior of the compulsive/relentless worker and binge/bulimic worker types. They think they are responsible for everything, communicate insufficiently, suppress their emotions and are not able to recognise the feelings and needs of their co-workers or to deal out praise or recognition. Instead, they intimidate others and demand that they adhere to their 'inhumane' standards and work long hours and frantically. This leads to a decline of morale and an increase of psychological and physical exhaustion for employees (see Robinson 2000, p. 214 ff., see Robinson 2014, p 149 f.). The quality of the group result is strongly endangered and compromised (see Fassel 1990, p. 83, see Fassel 1994, p. 108). Based on his experiences, Robinson has developed the following portrait of a workaholic superior:

- 'Constantly watches over employees' shoulders to monitor their work, while refusing to delegate
- Constantly pushes and hurries employees to the point where they feel undue stress and burnout
- Makes unreasonable demands in terms of work hours, workloads, and deadlines
- Has unpredictable, erratic moods, so employees never know what to expect
- Creates a climate of frenzy, urgency, and tension without respect for the feelings or personal lives of employees
- Manages time inefficiently because of overscheduling and overcommitting
- Judges himself or herself and employees without mercy as they struggle to hit impossible targets
- Tends to be overly critical and intolerant of even the most minor employee mistakes.' (Robinson 2014, p. 151)

In the evaluation of the work absences risk factor, an analysis of the group and the superiors respectively is recommended, as to their workaholic behavioural characteristics. A sole concentration on ill or absent employees seems pointless, and not very effective, if the reasons for the absences can be traced back to a workaholic co-worker or superior.

c) Further human resources risks

Motivation risk in terms of holding back performance
Excessive demand from a workaholic superior may trigger in employees the reaction of 'internal resignation'. Instead of fulfilling their tasks, they might be preoccupied with covering up mistakes and simulating successes. They often enter a state of passive resistance to, on the one hand, protect themselves and, on the other hand, to deliberately lower their own performance levels to harm the superior (see Robinson 2000, p. 218, see Robinson 2014, p. 152).

Peer to peer pressure
The risk of being ostracised by colleagues seems particularly high with the savouring workaholic, the anorexic workaholic as well as the attention-deficit workaholic. When tasks are delayed, deadlines neglected, or the group result is in danger as the fault of the workaholic, one should consider that the peer-to-peer-pressure process may be initialised by the colleagues, as shown in Section 3.2.

3.4.2 Human resources risks in regard to the workaholic

a) Bottleneck risk

The health complaints in the advanced stage of workaholism have been portrayed in Section 2.4. and are valid for all types of workaholism.

b) Professional development risk

There is the example of a time management seminar, which a workaholic is supposed to attend to optimise his personal time management. For the savouring workaholic, the anorexic workaholic, as well as the attention-deficit workaholic, such a seminar would probably bring no success, as the cause of the bad time management is manifested within the addiction. It is a component of the addicted behaviour and is basically needed for the adrenaline rush. A change in this behaviour could only be achieved through therapy. Further examples are personnel development programmes, which cannot be continued when the workaholic leaves the company.

c) Resignation risk

The fluctuation risk should be set higher especially for the attention-deficit workaholic. They tend to commence many projects, but not finish them. If they do not see the opportunity to satisfy this inclination within a company, they see transferring to a different company as adequate, to feed their addiction there.

In this context, the resignation risk is not necessarily seen as a negative, if the company is spared more significant damage by it. The effort to assess this risk will tendentially not justify the benefits. It, should however, be mentioned for completeness sake.

d) Adjustment risk

As all types of workaholism are governed in their actions by addiction, workaholics will presumably find it hard to adjust to their environment, and to changed framework conditions, and to adjust their performance. The effort to assess this risk will tendentially not justify the benefits. It should, however, be mentioned for completeness sake.

e) Motivation risk

The anorexic workaholic, as well as the attention-deficit workaholic, carries a motivation risk, as they hold back their performance as a manifestation of their addiction, and either work to the minimal optimum or begin various tasks without finishing them. The effort to assess this risk will tendentially not justify the benefits. It should, however, be mentioned for completeness sake.

f) Wrong decisions

All types of workaholism harbour the risk of wrong decisions, but they differ, as per the type of addiction, in the level of manifestation. Impatience and sudden episodes of working frantically can lead the compulsive/relentless worker and the binge/bulimic worker to make wrong decisions, as there is no time for adequate research. With the anorexic workaholic, the risk of making wrong decisions lies in the fact that he has put off work for a long time and then rushes through it in a frenzy. With the attention-deficit workaholic, this is, amongst other things, due to a lack of care in work preparation and work completion. For the savouring workaholic, the risk lies in him often losing sight, through a constant delay in progress, of what is essential, and he therefore is no longer able to make the right decision. Wrong decisions can, depending on company size and the importance of the decision, endanger the very existence of a company.

3.5 Concluding discussion

The following table contains an overview of the human resources risks and their impact on the group (G) and on the workaholic himself (W).

Table 6: Human resources risks by types of workaholism

Types of workaholism / **Human resources risks**	**Compulsive/ relentless workaholic/ binge/bulimic workaholic**		**Anorexic workaholic**		**Attention-deficit workaholic**		**Savouring workaholic**	
Consequences:	G	W	G	W	G	W	G	W
Bottleneck risk	●	●		●		●		●
Resignation risk	●					●		
Adjustment risk		●		●		●		●
Motivation risk	●			●		●		●
Management risk	●		●		●		●	
Wrong decisions	●	●		●		●		●
Peer to peer pressure	●		●		●		●	
Professional development risks		●		●		●		●

(Source: Meißner 2005, p. 127 Own illustration)

It can be established that the compulsive/relentless workaholic, and the binge/bulimic workaholic, obviously pose a high human resources risk for a company, especially if they work in the role of a superior. The risks on the employee level, complemented by the attention-deficit workaholic, are to be seen as accordingly high.

4 Empirical assessment

The aim of this chapter is to empirically investigate and discuss the theoretical findings introduced in Chapters 2 and 3. The investigation builds upon the analysis of a standardised questionnaire, completed by workaholic individuals.

The content of the empirical examination falls into the following focal topics:

- In this study, as described by Robinson and Fassel, the types of workaholics, and the characteristics and symptoms of workaholism, are to be verified for the German speaking world. This takes place in the form of a comparison with the 2005 study conducted by Meißner from the point of view of human resources departments, as well as of the evaluation of the current study.
- An evaluation of how operational influences may affect the development and promotion of workaholism. This will also be in comparison with the 2005 study.
- An analysis on to what extent workaholics themselves rate the effects of their workaholic behaviour on the business.

The objective of the survey is to analyse whether the theories introduced in Chapters 2 and 3 are verified by workaholics and, building on that, to deduce an adequate risk evaluation for the potential of the emergence of workaholism in the company. The questionnaire was deliberately customised to match the questionnaire of the 2005 study, so that the results could be directly compared. In Section 4.1., the research concept is introduced. The presentation of the empirical results following that are broken down into the individual theses with their respective evaluations.

4.1 Research concept

Due to lacking official recognition of workaholism as an illness, there is also a lack of a clear scale on which to measure the addiction quantitatively. Therefore, the examination of workaholism in this study limits itself to the qualitative level. On the basis of the qualitative dimension of the research subject, the scientific approach of explorative research will be applied to this study. It goes beyond the mere description of circumstances and aims for the discovery of new phenomena. Furthermore, it offers impulses for the development of new theses and theories. Explorative research is not governed by strict methodological rules, meaning that the results of this study are, from a scientific point of view, of a preliminary character in principle, as the theses formed are not reviewed quantitatively. In addition, they are not representative,[17] as the sample does not constitute a miniature representation of a defined entirety (see Uhl 1997, p. 5, see Stigler 2001, p. 23). An empirical-analytical approach was chosen as the scientific theoretical basis. In this context, empirical means that the findings are based on experience, observation, interviews and experiments. Analytical means that the research subject is dismantled into its components and the relationship of those components to one another is theoretically reconstructed (see Stigler 2001, p. 1 f.). The empirical-analytical approach often yields quantitative results. However, as the findings on workaholism are based on the experience and observations of therapists and consultants, and are therefore qualitative in character, the empirical analytical approach will be applied to this project, to determine qualitative results. This puts the focus on the possibility of the general occurrence of workaholism and not a certain probability of a quantitative occurrence. This also applies to the theses brought forward in this research concept.[18]

4.1.1 Defining objectives and determining indicators

Theory has determined economic and human resources consequences that can be traced back to workaholism. Meißner's 2005 study contained a first empirical description. In Chapters 2–3, theoretical bases[19] of workaholism were described and analysed, attempting a linguistic reconstruction of the relationship between workaholism and economics and human resources. They provide a fundamental orientation and determine which aspects are to be made the subject of this research, as well as providing conceptual reference systems.

The fundamental theoretical statement of this empirical study is therefore as follows:

Workaholism has economic and human resources consequences for the business. The objective of the empirical analysis is a description of the practice from the perspective of a workaholic on the basis of the theoretical principles.

This empirical study is a continuation of the 2005 investigation of the topic of workaholism from an economic and human resources perspective. It is

17 By representativeness Stigler means: 'There is a congruency between the theoretically defined totality and the actual totality represented by the samples provided; or: The sample is a miniature representation of a defined entirety.' (Stigler 2001, p. 23).

18 For qualitative research, see, amongst others, Lamnek 1995.

19 Stigler defines the theory as '… a system of logically consistent statements about a research subject.' (Stigler 2001, p. 19).

still necessary to limit the study to the investigation type[20] of description and to establish how workaholics themselves describe their form of workaholism, how they assess operational influences as promoting workaholism, and how they assess the operational consequences, they cause due to their disease. With this information, a presumable qualitative current state is generated, which will be interpreted accordingly and, where appropriate, possible diagnoses will be derived. The object of investigation will be specified as follows:

- Qualitative description and interpretation of the general indicators of workaholism
- Qualitative description and interpretation of the operational influences on the development or promotion of workaholism respectively
- Qualitative description and interpretation of the consequences of workaholic behaviour on business from the point of view of the affected workaholics

The indicators show to what extend the issue of workaholism indirectly relates to reality.[21] On the basis of this information, these theses are examined and interpreted in qualitative terms. As indicators of the research subject, the following items are consulted:

a) Indications of workaholism

These indicators relate to the description of workaholism traits. They were formulated in Chapter 2 in the presentation of the symptoms, the characteristics and the types of workaholism. Building on that, there follows a corresponding human resources risk analysis.

b) Operational influences

Against the theoretical background that operational influences may promote workaholism, indicators are raised, which refer to influences through colleagues

---

20 Fritz and Helene Karmasin differentiate between the following examination categories: description (A description of the fact), diagnosis (Individual observational statements not requiring a strict explanation. Via the symptoms, statements are made on the significance of the circumstances of a specific space-time-area, whereby the experiences of the evaluator also come into the diagnosis. The more symptoms, the higher the probability of the correctness of the diagnosis.) Explanation (answer to the cause of a specific issue), prognosis (forecast for the occurrence of a certain issue) (see Karmasin/Karmasin 1977, p. 47 ff.).

21 If workaholism were medically recognised, the facts of the addictions would be directly relating to reality. One would talk about constructs then and not indicators, which then relate indirectly to reality (see Stigler 2001, p. 19).

and management as well as through operational framework conditions. Questions were specifically about working hour models, work behaviours and the workers' fears; from those risks were derived.

c) Impacts of workaholic behaviour on the business

The economic and human resources consequences of workaholism were determined in Sections 3.3. and 3.4. In the empirical survey, the direct indicator with regard to the topic 'sick leave' was determined. Indirect indicators can be derived from the items of workaholism indications and operational influences on the promotion of workaholism, as well as via the self-assessment of workaholics with regard to the impact of their behaviour on the business.

4.1.2 Target group identification and sample size

When workaholism is discussed in public, primarily workaholics are depicted as people who- to put it simply - work too much. The Workaholics Anonymous groups, business consultants and psychologists, however, have ascertained that the illness is by far more complex, and can manifest in a variety of different forms. An example of the different forms can be seen in the work of a variety of researchers on the topic of workaholism:

- Robinson is a family therapist who gathered his experience with workaholism through various case studies from his own professional practice.
- Fassel collected her experiences in her long-standing career as a business consultant, during which she has been confronted with numerous workaholics.
- Poppelreuter has, as a psychologist, in his dissertation, for the first time in Germany carried out an empirical study in the form of a questionnaire, in which workaholics and non-workaholics were asked about the symptoms of workaholism.
- Heide's findings result from the observation of members of Workaholics Anonymous groups, as well as from a long-term examination of the topic as a professor of social economy.

Due to the lack of medical recognition of workaholism, and the research still being in its infancy, it is still difficult to clearly define when a person is a workaholic, or simply a person who works a lot. Resulting from this are the corresponding challenges to define an adequate target group for research projects.

This is also evident in the following research works, which only under great difficulty, and by using theoretical tools, were able to determine their group of test subjects.

In a commentary on her 2008 study, Städele elaborates that, due to the lack of reliable diagnoses of workaholism, it is difficult to define a target group and to reach those affected by workaholism. For that reason, she carried out an ex-post-facto study, in which she gathered her findings through the comparison of extreme groups. The test groups were only determined by means of an artificial criterion after the data collection. At a basis, she used as a measuring tool Schneider's scale for the recording of work relatedness (SEA), which Schneider developed in his 2001 dissertation with the University of Würzburg (see Schneider 2001). This scale consists of 20 items attributed to workaholism to be answered with a Yes/No selection. Each 'Yes' reply is awarded a point as an indicator for workaholism. The probability of the presence of workaholism is calculated by adding up the points.

The classification of workaholic and non-workaholic survey participants followed through the division of the total sample into four quartiles. 25 % of the people surveyed with the highest SEA-expression were regarded as workaholic, the 25 % with the lowest SEA-expression were regarded as non-workaholic. The remaining 50 % of those surveyed were disregarded (see Städele 2008, p. 69ff.). Städele herself elaborates that her survey does not present the actual markedness of individual persons on the workaholism scale, but simply examines the differences in markedness between classified workaholics and non-workaholics. It is, thus, an examination of the relative position of the comparative groups. Therefore, no statements are possible on whether the subjects in this examination were actual workaholics or not (see Städele 2008, p. 71).

Vicario, in 2013, chose the same survey form as Städele as the basis for her study, but concentrated on the workaholism issue in the helping services professions. Matthey, when surveying the professional group of journalists in 2011, also chose this method (see Badura 2013).

In her 2006 study, Voigt chose a differentiated approach. She raised two samples, on which her study is based: On the one hand, she created a group of workaholics from members of the self-help group Workaholics Anonymous and an equivalent control group, representing the group of non-workaholics.

On the other hand, all test subjects, in addition, filled out Schneider's questionnaire on the recording of work relatedness, creating a second sample. Both these samples (a total of 18 test subjects) then became the subject of her analysis, in which she examined, using questionnaires and semi-structured interviews, to what extent specific personality traits can be assigned to workaholics, and whether there are formative role models which have promoted workaholism.

In the empirical survey at hand, the assumption was made for the purpose of determining a target group that people who voluntarily and regularly attend Workaholics Anonymous meetings, fulfil a sufficient criterion that the phenomenon of workaholism exists and that it has caused personal problems for those affected. Therefore, for the first time in the German speaking area, an investigation was performed, questioning exclusively self-confessed workaholics on the topic with an economic and human resources focus.

When determining the sample, a regional limitation was put on it, containing only the countries Germany, Austria and Switzerland. The selection criterion was defined as workaholics regularly attending Workaholics Anonymous meetings. The questionnaire was sent by email to all 28 Workaholics Anonymous groups in Germany, to the group in Switzerland and to all four groups in Austria. The subjective views of the test subjects reflect an expert opinion which cannot be evaluated by objective assessment criteria.

The questionnaires were sent out in May 2015 via email. An internet link led the test subjects to the questions, which could be answered quickly and comfortably online. A total of 33 emails were sent to the Workaholics Anonymous groups involved, who, in turn, circulated the email among the members of their group via email. This procedure did not make it clear what the total number is of those affected, as this was an anonymous working group. 21 questionnaires were answered (n = 21), the percentage of useable questionnaires within the sample (n = 17) is 81 %. Four questionnaires could not be used, mainly because the questions had not been answered in full. In spite of this, descriptive and diagnostic statements, where appropriate, should be possible on a qualitative level on the basis of this empirical data. Only three questionnaires came back from Austria and Switzerland, so that a country specific evaluation would have made no sense. To support the survey results, 23 case studies published in German language media were evaluated, in which workaholics described their illness, their work behaviour and the impact on their families. This increases the sample with corresponding questions to a total of n= 40 and will also be consulted in the eligible evaluations as an expansion of the sample, and for the validation of the survey results. The expanded sample will be used for the purpose of the evaluation under the term 'cumulative analysis'.

4.1.3 List of theses, questionnaire and data analysis

The overview of the current state of workaholism research in Germany, as described in the introduction, clearly shows that the research in the German speaking area is still in its infancy. An empirical examination of the findings of psychologists and consultants is still outstanding. This study marks the first step towards evaluating and describing the typical behavioural traits of workaholics from the perspective of those affected. Because it is still very early on in the research, this step of a descriptive representation seems necessary, to gather deeper insights from the point of view of workaholics. Therefore, the following theses have been formulated on the basis of expert knowledge (see Chapter 2). These theses describe traits of workaholism, which are to be investigated through an analysis of the empirical examination.

Thesis 1	*Workaholism affects people irrespective of gender and age.*
Thesis 2	*Workaholism primarily affects people with academic degrees and is specifically a managerial disease.*
Thesis 3	Indications of workaholism.
Thesis 3.1	*The indications for workaholism in the form of characteristics, symptoms and types of workaholism, identified by psychologists and consultants, have been confirmed by the test subjects.*
Thesis 3.2	*Workaholics neglect their health.*
Thesis 3.3	*Workaholics have a higher number of work absences.*
Thesis 3.4	*The attendance of the support group Workaholics Anonymous has a positive effect on the severity of the illness.*
Thesis 3.5	*The properties of the compulsive/relentless type of workaholism are more prevalent than those of the remaining types.*
Thesis 4	*Operational influences on the development and promotion of workaholism.*
Thesis 4.1	*Workaholism is caused by or promoted by operational influences.*
Thesis 4.2	*Management have a decisive influence on the development or promotion of workaholism.*
Thesis 5	*Operational consequences of workaholism were assessed as less negative in the self-assessment of workaholics.*

The topic of workaholism is quite complicated for the reasons listed above. For this reason, the data collection method of the quantitative interview in the form of a standardised questionnaires was selected.[22] This gave those surveyed the opportunity to respond to the questions self-critically under the

22 For the advantages and disadvantages of a written versus an oral survey see Richter 1969, p. 27 ff. and Stigler 2001, p. 33 ff.

umbrella of anonymity, without being exposed to the pressure and the stress of a personal interview.

The questionnaire was divided into thematic blocks according to the theses. The questions are introduced in detail during the data analysis of the respective Thesis. As an examination method, a verbal rating scale[23] was selected. The test subjects who were surveyed were given a scale, on which they could mark the degree of manifestation of a characteristic in case of an object or the degree of their acceptance of a statement (see Karmasin/Karmasin 1977, p. 96). Apart from the Yes/No-replies, there were four possible answer categories. The middle level was deliberately left out, to avoid irritation in the interpretation of the evaluation. It allows for several meanings: a 'middle of the road' reply, a 'don't know'-reply, an irrelevant reply or a protest reply (see Stigler 2001, p. 38).

Table 7 depicts an overview of the groups and question complexes.

Table 7: Overview of thematic groups and question topics

1 Questions about the person	2 Health issues	3 Questions about working behaviour
• Gender • Age • Employment Type • Profession	• Days of absences • Severity level of the symptoms of workaholism • Identification of workaholism	• Severity level of typical workaholic behaviour

4 Questions about the emergence of work addiction	5 Questions about effects on the company	6 Remarks of respondents
• Performance pressure • Fun at work • Fears about work • Consequences of workaholism • Practiced working time model	• Self-assessment of the impact of personal workaholic behaviour on companies	• Possible support options

(Source: Own illustration)

23 Applied rating scale with the degree of manifestation: 'occurs very frequently, occurs frequently, rarely occurs, never occurs'.

Due to the qualitative and descriptive character of the evaluation, the data analysis is restricted to the allocation of frequency in percentage. Further evaluations, such as determining an average value or standard deviation would be hardly informative and would offer no grounds for serious interpretation due to the small total sample. As the objective of this empirical study is a fundamental qualitative description of workaholism indicators as well as of addiction-causing-or-promoting operational influences, a degree of spread grounded in a binary evaluation of 'does occur/does not occur', is defined, in addition to the degree of manifestation on the basis of a verbal rating scale.

To determine the value 'does occur', the degree of manifestation 'occurs very frequently/occurs frequently' has been added. The value 'rarely occurs/never occurs' is equivalent to the degree of spread 'does not occur'.

With the degree of spread comes the opportunity to analyse to what extent the respective indicators are present with the test subjects. The degree of manifestation also makes it possible to achieve a qualitative estimate of a possible probability of frequency or a risk evaluation.

4.2 Empirical data analysis

In the following chapter, the questionnaires are analysed in terms of workaholism indicators, operational influences on the development and promotion respectively of workaholism, as well as the self-assessment of the impact of personal workaholic behaviour on companies.

4.2.1 Indications of workaholism

Thesis 1	*Workaholism affects people irrespective of gender and age.*

Personal details:
At the beginning of the questionnaire are general questions on personal details, the purpose of which is to be able to make a possible differentiation between the sexes. 65 % of the test subjects were women and 35 % were men. This clearly shows that both sexes can be affected by workaholism. It becomes even clearer in the cumulative evaluation, together with the case studies, where the distribution is 53 % men and 48 % women. Thus, it is clear that the outbreak of the illness does not depend on gender.

If one looks at the previous studies in comparison, this thesis is also confirmed:

Table 8: Gender distribution compared to further studies

Gender	Meißner 2017 (n=17)	Meißner, incl. case studies 2017 (n=40)	Städele 2008 (n=111)	Vicario 2013 (n=89)
male	35 %	53 %	43 %	22 %
female	65 %	48 %	57 %	78 %

(Source: Own illustration, Städele 2008, p. 81, Vicario 2013, p. 78)

The strikingly high number of female test subjects in Vicario's study most likely has to do with the study concentrating on the so called 'helping professions', where generally more women belong to the workforce.

The required age groups were all present, whereby the most noticeable age groups, with 29 % each, were the group of the 41 – 50-year-olds and of the 51 – 60-year olds. This confirms the assumption that workaholism is a slow process and increasingly breaks out only after 10-20 years of professional life. These numbers were confirmed by the cumulative evaluation, with only marginal deviations.

Table 9: Age distribution in the 2017 study compared to case studies

Age	Meißner 2017 (n=17)	Meißner, incl. case studies 2017 (n=40)
< 20 = no information	0 %	12 %
20–30	6 %	5 %
31–40	18 %	20 %
41–50	29 %	25 %
51–60	29 %	28 %
> 60	18 %	10 %

(Source: Own illustration)

Thesis 2	*Workaholism primarily affects people with academic degrees and is specifically a managerial disease.*

Of those surveyed, 71 % stated that they worked as salaried employees and were therefore operating in a company environment. Only 18 % of those surveyed were self-employed. The cumulative evaluation confirmed the numbers with 80 % in dependent employment and 10 % self-employed.

The studies published by Städele and Vicario show the same tendencies:

Table 10: Employment status compared to further studies

Employment status	**Meißner 2017 (n=11)**	**Meißner, incl. case studies 2017 (n=40)**	**Städele 2008 (n=111)**	**Vicario 2013 (n=89)**
no information	11 %	10 %	31 %	8 %
self-employed	18 %	10 %	9 %	4 %
salaried employee	71 %	80 %	60 %	88 %

(Source: Own illustration, Städele 2008, p. 81, Vicario 2013, p. 78)

The small number of self-employed is surprising, especially as this professional group is suspected of working more than salaried employees to ensure their personal existence and that of their family. This may be an indication that the amount of hours worked does not necessarily stand in connection with workaholism.

Conclusion:
The high number of workaholics in dependent employment is a clear indication for companies that there is a high probability of them having a workaholic among their staff. Companies should approach this responsibility and risk with an appropriate human resources risk management strategy, to identify those affected and support them in a goal-oriented fashion.

47 % of those surveyed had an academic qualification, 35 % had a non-academic qualification, 18 % did not provide information on this. Cumulatively, with the case studies, this makes an academics quota of 63 %. From this can be deduced a cautious slight tendency towards a confirmation of the thesis, that specifically employees with higher qualifications could be affected by workaholism more than non-academically qualified employees. If one looks at Vicario's and Voigt's studies, this cautious tendency is confirmed.

Conclusion:
People with academic degrees pose a slightly higher risk group. Companies can use this finding as a prioritising aid.

Table 11: Academic degrees compared to further studies

Academic degree	Meißner 2017 (n=11)	Meißner, incl. case studies 2017 (n=40)	Städele 2008 (n=111)	Vicario 2013 (n=89)	Voigt 2006 (n=8)
academic	47 %	63 %	45 %	53 %	87 %
non- academic	35 %	25 %	55 %	47 %	13 %
no information	18 %	12 %	0 %	0 %	0 %

(Source: Own illustration, Städele 2008, p. 81, Vicario 2013, p. 78, Voigt 2006, p. 87)

What becomes apparent in this study, however, is that workaholism is not the issue of specific professions, but runs through all professions. 24 % of those surveyed were teachers/school psychologists, 12 % secretaries, followed by the professions nurse, production planner, aged-care nurse, human resources manager, film makers/press - and public relations. No management executives took part in the study. Among the case studies, however, eight people were listed in executive positions (manager, managing director, care facility director), equalling a cumulative quota of 20 %. Also represented were professions like laboratory technicians, financial advisers, engineers, programmers, and people working in insurance and administration.

The large variety of professions proves that workaholism is not restricted to specific professional groups, even if a tendency towards teachers/school psychologists and management executives may suggest otherwise.

The thesis that workaholism more often affects people with academic degrees, was put forward in this investigation. It could, however, neither be confirmed nor disproved that workaholism primarily affects managers and therefore is effectively a managerial disease.

Conclusion:
Even if the study has not provided proof that workaholism explicitly is a management phenomenon, from a business point of view the group of managers should be prioritised in risk assessment, as they usually constitute key figures for companies and therefore have a corresponding influence on the achievement of corporate goals and results.

Questions on symptoms/illnesses affecting workaholics:

Thesis 3	Indications of Workaholism.
Thesis 3.1	*The indication for workaholism in the form of characteristics, symptoms and types of workaholism, identified by psychologists and consultants, have been confirmed by the test subjects.*

Thesis 3.2	*Workaholics neglect their health.*
Thesis 3.3	*Workaholics have a higher number of work absences.*

Fundamentally, this part of the study was trying to prove that workaholics neglect their health and are aware of it. For this purpose, the following question was posed:

'Have you neglected your health?'

94 % of those surveyed confirmed this. This suggests that a clear bottleneck risk for companies exists, as soon as a person's neglected health manifests as an illness, leading to absences from work.

The average number of days those surveyed were absent from work was 4.5 days per year. If compared to the German national average of 9.5 days per year in 2014 (see German Federal Statistical Office 2016, sickness levels), this lies significantly below the average. None of the test subjects was absent from work for more than 10 days per year.

The neglect of their health, in this study, therefore does not manifest in actual work absences for test subjects. The reasons for this could be manifold:

- The test subjects have reduced their health problems so far, through actively combatting their addiction, that they no longer manifest as work absences
- Potential fears in the test subjects lead to attending work, even when sick, although they really should have stayed at home.

The thesis that workaholics neglect their health can be deemed as very likely true after this study, and can be seen as confirmed. However, there is no evidence that workaholics at the same time have a high number of work absences; here, rather the opposite became apparent and the thesis was therefore not confirmed.

Conclusion:
From this, one can draw the careful conclusion that companies should not neglect the analysis of short term illnesses in their workaholic risk identification, and probe more deeply on this issue, to get to the bottom of the reasons for work absences.

This takes more effort and above all a structured and professional approach in the analysis of absences within the company. As part of the corporate duty of care for the sustainable retention of work force, this should be self-evident. Of course, this does not exempt the company from the necessity of analysing the causes of long time illnesses nonetheless, as the later examination of the illnesses affecting workaholics will clearly show.

To survey the physical and behavioural symptoms according to Fassel and Robinson, the following question was posed (see Figure 4):

'Which of the following symptoms of workaholism have you had?'

With 47 % each, the symptoms unrest, tension as well as disrupted sleep/inability to relax were ticked as occurring very frequently. With 41 %, followed mood swings (euphoria/depression/mental illnesses). If one looks at the cumulative evaluation from 'occurs very frequently and frequently' the most prominent symptoms were as follows:

- Unrest with 94 %,
- Tension with 88 %,
- Disrupted sleep/inability to relax with 82 %,
- Mood swings (euphoria/depression/mental illnesses), concentration problems, irritability and impatience as well as permanent exhaustion with 76 % each,
- Forgetfulness with 71 %,
- Hyperactivity with 65 %,
- Digestive problems with 53 % and
- Acute hearing loss/tinnitus, headaches and back pain with 41 % each.

Conclusion:
In this context, it becomes clear that the symptoms obviously can be divided into two groups: The group >50 % mainly contains symptoms, which require rather less medical attention, while the symptoms < 50 % generally speaking are more likely to require medical treatment.

The cumulative analysis together with the case studies, in this context, yield only limited validation opportunities, as the illnesses were merely described in isolation. Nonetheless, two symptoms of workaholism can be pinpointed, which go beyond the results of the investigation and tendentially validate them through the case studies:

Because of their similarity, the points 'disrupted sleep' and 'the inability to relax' from the survey were grouped together with the point 'thoughts always revolve around work' from the case studies, where it was named significantly often. This results in a cumulative result of 63 % of the test subjects, to be associated with this point; the survey of the Workaholics Anonymous had had the result 82 % for this point.

The second symptom, mood swings (euphoria/depression/mental illnesses) was grouped together with the point burnout from the case studies, which had been mentioned strikingly often in those. This leads to a cumulative result of 53 % allocated to this point.

Yet, one has to differentiate at this point. The low level of absences among the test subjects is an indicator that they are not ill to the point where they cannot work, or have not called in sick and were able to continue working. In the case studies, however, burnout had been named directly, usually accompanied by the inability to work. Therefore, it can be deduced that workaholics do not necessarily have a high level of work absences, but, in an inversion of the argument, one can say that certain long-time illnesses (for example burnout) point towards the presence of workaholism.

It should be noted that, in the current study, the experience of psychologists is represented, in which workaholic individuals often undergo therapy for psychological illnesses and depression (see Fassel 1994, p. 71).

Interesting in this context is the result that in the analysis of the case studies, with one exception, exclusively men were affected by 'burnout' (6 mentions) and only one man explicitly mentioned his participation in Workaholics Anonymous meetings. For the remaining men, there is no information on this, and one can only assume that they either do not actually go to these meetings or do not want to make their attendance public.

If one looks at the symptoms according to gender, no significant differences can be detected.

Conclusion:
From a company perspective, this tentatively calls for a further prioritisation of the identification of workaholism in companies. It has been worked out that, according to this study, from a company point of view, a more prominent group of employees may have emerged: male, academically qualified employees in management positions, affected by long-term illness. This approach, however, is merely to be seen as an aid in demonstrating how a prioritisation for a risk analysis as part of a risk assessment can be carried out. This is not to draw a conclusion that this study has provided proof that one group of employees is deemed to be specifically prone, or that workaholism would only occur within it. Also, the recommendation is made not to differentiate managers by gender, when carrying out a risk analysis. This form of analysis of work absences is therefore an addition to the necessity introduced above to examine short-term illnesses.

If one compares the statements of those affected with the empirical survey from 2005 (see Figure 4), in which human resources managers were asked which illnesses occurred within companies, one can ascertain that the illnesses acute hearing loss/tinnitus, headaches and back pain were represented with more than 50 % (see Meißner 2005, p. 144). In the current survey, these points are indicated, at 41 % each, as occurs very frequently/occurs frequently. This is, at least, an indicator and a lead for companies, that these illnesses can also occur with workaholics. It is therefore advisable to investigate especially thoroughly

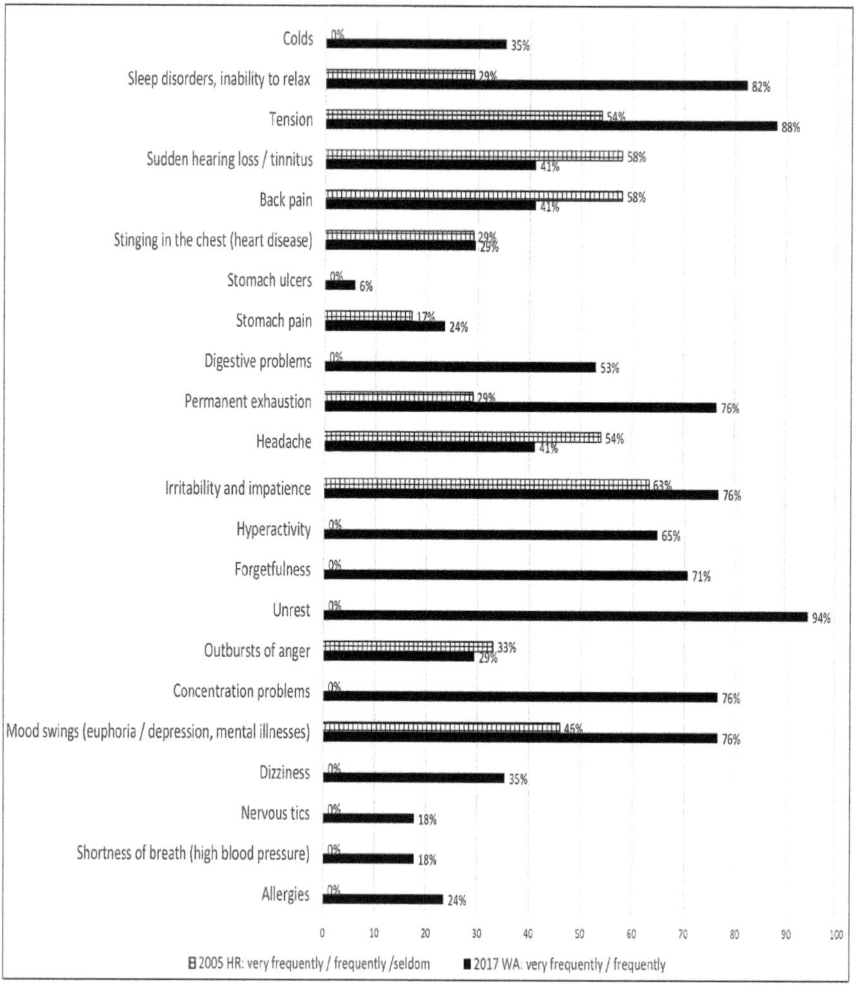

Figure 4: Comparison of symptoms 2017 (Workaholics) with 2005 study (Human Resources Departments)

(Source: Own illustration)

the development of these illnesses in sickness analyses within a company, and to identify further workaholism criteria, if applicable. It is interesting that the companies have listed irritability and impatience at 63 % on the list of observed behaviours and that this sentiment has been confirmed at 76 % in the current survey. Therefore, one cannot just identify this point, as is common practice, as a mood barometer for corporate culture, but one must also consider it as an indicator for workaholism.

In addition, the symptom of tension, which in 2005 was put at 54 % by the human resources departments, can also be identified as a symptom of workaholism. In the current survey, 88 % of those surveyed have confirmed this point.

From a corporate point of view, it can be established that the analyses of causes of the exemplary tension, back pain and headaches or acute hearing loss in relation to workaholism have fallen short to date. As the 2005 study has shown, these illnesses are present within companies, but are not connected with workaholism. As these symptoms were, however, confirmed as an indicator, companies have to ask themselves at this point how they can widen their perspective on illness analysis. Corporate illness analysis is often carried out only on the basis of concrete days of absence, and maybe interviews of employees returning after an illness or operational integration management, which is a special German law requirement. But as the investigation has indicated, the most common symptoms are clearly not obvious for companies from the amount of work absences.

Conclusion:
Hence, there is a necessity for companies to develop a system for the identification and analysis of observed behaviours in personnel indicative of workaholism (such as unrest, tension, mood swings, irritability/impatience, exhaustion, forgetfulness, hyperactivity). These aspects are often already part of company employee surveys, for example on topics such as employee satisfaction and corporate culture, and from there could become part of an analysis of workaholism.[24]

Given the analysis of the illnesses, it seems appropriate at this point to ask whether there may be a connection between the severity of the illness and the regular participation in Workaholics Anonymous meetings.

---

24 See risk analysis of symptoms in Chapter 5.2. as well as the recommendations for action in Chapter 6.

This is expressed in the following thesis:

Thesis 3.4	*The attendance of the support group Workaholics Anonymous has a positive effect on the severity of the illness.*

To this end, one should take a closer look at the following two questions.

'How did you realise you were a workaholic?'

In reply, 41 % of those surveyed stated that they realised they were workaholic based on their awareness of their own psychological illnesses. 29 % came to that awareness on the basis of physical illnesses. Only 12 % were diagnosed with workaholism by their physician on the basis of physical illness, and only 6 % on the basis of psychological illness, although double entries were permitted here. One test subject declared that he realised he was a workaholic through his own awareness and through his physician. In the cumulative study with the case studies, 55 % of test subjects realised themselves that they were workaholics, and 28 % were brought to this realisation via their physicians. These deviations may have been caused by the severity of the disease, as the example of burnout shows. This illness plays only a minor role in the current study, but played a very significant role in the case studies.

It remains unclear why so few cases have been diagnosed by physicians. Are doctors not sufficiently trained to diagnose workaholism? Are medical practitioners reluctant to make the respective diagnosis because of the addiction not being officially recognised? Are those affected afraid of admitting to their workaholism in front of their doctors? Have those surveyed, who recognised their addictive behaviour through self-awareness, fortunately not reached such an advanced stage yet that they are severely ill and need medical help? The last point, at least, seems to be tendentially confirmed in this study, as shown in the analysis of the symptoms.

'Do you regularly take part in Workaholic Anonymous meetings to overcome workaholism?'

Due to the nature of the selection of test subjects, this question was answered with Yes by 82 % of the test subjects. In the cumulative study, 68 % of test subjects were identified as actively taking part in Workaholics Anonymous meetings.

The high level of regular attendance at the meetings, in combination with low work absences, may allow for the conclusion that there is a positive correlation between the timely recognition of the addiction and asking for help in relation to the severity of the illness. The survey results of this study support that severe medical illnesses occur rather more uncommonly, and this thus implies that those affected get the appropriate help in time to get their workaholism under control.

In the following, it will be investigated how the severity of the illness correlates with the participation in Workaholics Anonymous meetings. To that end, the illnesses were allocated to the stages according to Fassel (see Fassel 1994, p. 71) in the following table, whereby this allocation is not to be seen as dogmatic, as there can always be variations in the severity of an illness.

Table 12: Allocation of illnesses to the stages of workaholism

Stages	**Illnesses/Effects of workaholism**
1. Early stage	Nervous tics
	Outbursts of anger
	Unrest
	Forgetfulness
	Hyperactivity
	Irritability and impatience
	Digestive problems
	Stomach pain
	Tension
	Colds and 'flu'
2. Middle stage	Allergies
	Concentration problems
	Headaches
	State of permanent exhaustion
	Back pain
	Acute hearing loss/tinnitus
	Sleep disorders, unable to relax
3. Final stage	High blood pressure (shortness of breath)
	Dizziness
	Stomach ulcers
	Mood swings, depression, severe mental illnesses
	Chest pain (heart disease)

(Source: Own illustration)

The weighted analysis (see Figure 5) allocating symptoms to the stages revealed that 39 % (cumulative analysis 33 %) of the symptoms are allocated to the early stage, 38 % (cumulative 39 %) to the middle stage and 23 % (cumulative 28 %) to the final stage. This means that 77 % of the symptoms displayed by the workaholics surveyed are located in the early and middle stages and tend to require only lighter medical treatment as opposed to those in the final stage. It is striking that the workaholism symptoms of those surveyed that have recognised by themselves that they were workaholics, are at 41 % (cumulative 40 %) located in the early stage, at 39 % (cumulative 40 %) in the middles stage, and only at 20 % (cumulative 20 %) in the final stage. Of the symptoms of those surveyed, who were put onto a diagnosis of workaholism by their physician, 33 % (cumulative 41 %) were situated in the final stage.

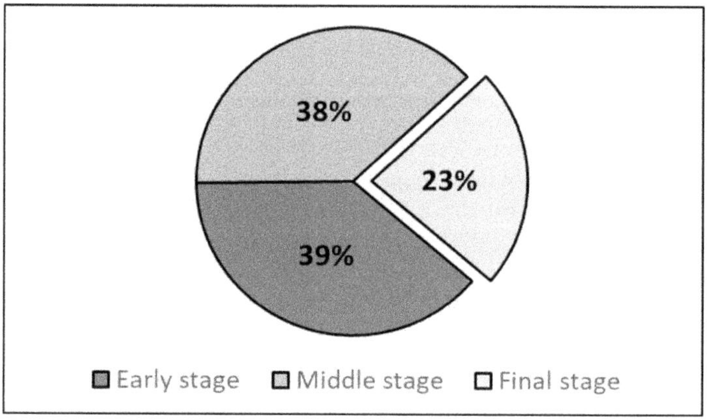

Figure 5: Allocation of the symptoms to the stages of workaholism
(Source: Own illustration)

Conclusion:
One can therefore tentatively derive the following conclusions from the results of the current study: The assessment through psychologists and experts generally followed from psychological/therapeutic treatment of workaholics. It can thus be assumed that the patients were already in a stage of the addiction, where they were afflicted by such a severity of illness that they required medical and psychological help. Whereas it is apparent from this study that the more severe illnesses, due to the low level of work absences, are not detected among

the members of Workaholics Anonymous. This may be an indication that the participants in this study are in the early or middle stages of the addiction and therefore do not largely present at psychologists' or medical practices. This makes evident the important significance of the Workaholics Anonymous groups: through the timely recognition of workaholism in the early/middle stage and the active utilisation of help from Workaholics Anonymous, severe illnesses in those affected may presumably be avoided, and the consequences of the addiction mitigated.

At the same time, by implication - in contrast to the recognised workaholic illnesses - it can be assumed that there is a very high hidden number of workaholic employees in business. This illustrates all the more clearly that there is an equally high requirement for corporate action to identify workaholics in a timely manner, in order to not only minimise the potential risk of work absences at a later stage of workaholism through timely treatment, but also to minimise or avoid all further human resources and economic consequences, such as fluctuation, demotivation, absences of colleagues, or wrong decisions.

Question on the characteristic behavioural traits of workaholics and the allocation to the types of workaholism:

In this evaluation, it is to be analysed to what extent the typical behaviour of workaholics as identified by therapists and psychologists actually matches the self-assessment of those affected and whether an allocation to the different types of workaholism can be detected.

This is expressed in the following thesis:

Thesis 3.5	*The properties of the compulsive/relentless type of workaholism are more prevalent than those of the remaining types.*

As an introduction, a question was chosen about the loss of control, a central characteristic of alcoholism:

'Have you lost control over your actions?'

This is confirmed by 71 % of those surveyed and therefore can be counted as a central characteristic from the point of view of those affected.

The itemisation of the typical characteristics, described in Chapter 2, was to be ascertained on the basis of the following question:

'The following descriptions mirror behaviours of workaholics. Which of these did you display and to what degree of manifestation?'

The cumulative evaluation 'occurs very frequently/occurs frequently' of the survey clearly showed the traits of workaholism in Table 13. Negation, in this context, means that the criterion of workaholism is fulfilled, if the statement is worded in the negative. Example: You are **not** interested in the work and in the outcome. To avoid one-sidedness, positive and negative statements were mixed together in the questionnaire for design purposes.

Of 20 typical behaviours, 12 could be identified at above 50 % respectively and thus actually confirmed by those affected. Of which 30 % with over 70 % respectively can be quite clearly identified. If one takes into account the tendential validation of the points 'moody' and 'work results not submitted on time' with 41 % each, the verification rate is at 70 %. This means that the behaviours observed by therapists and psychologists are actually also confirmed by those affected themselves, thus giving companies concrete indications for the identification of workaholic behaviour.

If one, at this point, compares the points 'you take work home' and 'you also work weekends or while on holiday' with 71 % each, one can see a clear correlation to the following question:

'Have you neglected your social environment (friends/family)?'

88 % of test subjects confirmed in this survey that they were, due to their workaholism, neglecting friends and/or family, 73 % in the cumulative analysis with the case studies. This high approximate correspondence with the above points 'you takework home' and 'you also work weekends or while on holiday' lets these behavioural patterns clearly stand out, and one can sense, going by the reports from the psychologists and therapists (see Chapter 2), which serious consequences workaholism has on private life. The cumulative analysis with the case studies, for the purpose of substantiation of the current survey, revealed that the points 'you are the first to arrive each day and the last to leave' (50 %) and 'an absolute flawless quality of work' (55 %) were more clearly detectable. Following that are the points 'you take work home' and 'you work weekends or while on holiday' with 43 % each.

In addition, it is striking that 76 % of those surveyed assessed themselves as 'Working well in a team with an eye for what is essential', but, at the same time, 53 % of them admit to, 'Excessively controlling their colleagues/co-workers, because they do not trust them to complete the tasks independently'. This is mirrored in the contradiction, which would probably be seen differently from the point of view of the colleagues and co-workers, as excessive control is usually not seen as particularly favourable.

Table 13: Workaholic behaviours

	Workaholic behavioural characteristics:	**(very) frequently/**	**Remarks**
1.	You are interested in the work and in the outcome (negation)	94 %	
2.	An absolutely flawless quality of work is your work requirement	88 %	validated
3.	You take on tasks, although you do not have to	88 %	validated
4.	You learn from mistakes (negation)	82 %	
5.	You work well in a team and have an eye for what is essential (negation)	76 %	
6.	You take work home	71 %	validated
7.	You work weekends or while on holiday	71 %	validated
8.	You seek new tasks, although not having completed old ones	71 %	validated
9.	You make creative contributions (negation)	71 %	
10.	Your day-to-day work is characterised by hectic and uncoordinated styles of work	59 %	validated
11.	Small talk about private matters does not take place, as you are solely fixated on work	59 %	validated
12.	You are the first to arrive each day and the last to leave	53 %	validated
13.	You do not tolerate work errors in others	53 %	validated
14.	You excessively control your colleagues/co-workers, because you do not trust them to be able to complete the tasks independently	53 %	validated
15.	You are able to delegate tasks (negation)	41 %	validated
16.	You are moody	41 %	tendency
17.	Work results are not submitted in time, for fear of them being faulty	41 %	tendency
18	Collaboration in the team is inhibited, as you are constantly raising new concerns	18 %	
19.	You take risks and also accept 80 %-solutions (negation)	18 %	validated
20.	You have outbursts of anger	18 %	

(Source: Own illustration)

Beyond the evaluated behaviours, the individual analysis of the case studies without the test subjects from the current survey indicates that 78 % of those affected orient their lives exclusively towards work and are troubled by a bad conscience and feelings of guilt when they are not working. These results complement and correlate with the investigation relating to the above question on the neglect of the social environment.

Further to this, 39 % of those affected remarked to have experienced work also as an intoxication with partial withdrawal symptoms and a compulsion to work. This matches the views of therapists and psychologists, as described in Chap 2.

The allocation of the types of workaholism according to the behavioural criteria has, for the sake of comparability, been adopted from the 2005 study (Meißner 2005, p. 153). It should be recalled at this stage that this allocation was done on the basis of descriptions of behaviours provided by therapists and psychologists and that the boundaries between the individual types are fluid and may not in any case be interpreted in a dogmatic fashion. The aim is merely to work out whether typical behaviour traits may be assigned to the types of workaholism.

As for the comparison with the 2005 study, it must be said that the criteria 'working on weekends', 'delegation', 'outbursts of anger', 'moody' and 'control of colleagues/co-workers' were newly added to the current study and can therefore not be compared.

In the 2005 study, a differentiation was made between employees and managers. As there were no managers involved in this survey, the current results are to be compared with the evaluation from human resources departments in 2005 (see Meißner 2005, p. 156 ff.) for the group of employees (see Table 15).

Type compulsive/relentless workaholic

14 questions are allocated to this type (see Table 14). Of which 12 questions are validated and one question tendentially validated. This result quite firmly confirms the type of the compulsive/relentless workaholic and therefore identifies it as a very prominent type of workaholism.

Table 14: Allocation of behaviours to the types of workaholism

	Workaholic behavioural characteristics	Compulsive	Savour	Binge	Deficit
1.	You are interested in the work and in the outcome (negation)		x		
2.	An absolutely flawless quality of work is your work requirement	xv	xv		
3.	You take on tasks, although you do not have to	xv			
4.	You learn from mistakes (negation)	xv	xv	xv	xv
5.	You work well in a team and have an eye for what is essential (negation)	xv	xv	xv	xv
6.	You take work home	xv			
7.	You work weekends and while on holiday	xv	xv		
8.	You seek new tasks, although not having completed old ones				xv
9.	You make creative contributions (negation)		x		
10.	Your day-to-day work is characterised by hectic and uncoordinated styles of work			xv	xv
11.	Small talk about private matters does not take place, as you are solely fixated on work	xv			
12.	You are the first to arrive each day and the last to leave	xv			
13.	You do not tolerate work errors in others	xv			
14.	You excessively control your colleagues/ co-workers, because you do not trust them to be able to complete the tasks independently	xv			
15.	You are able to delegate tasks (negation)	xv	xv	xv	
16.	You are moody	xtv			
17.	Work results are not submitted in time, for fear of them being faulty		xtv		
18	Collaboration in the team is inhibited, as you are constantly raising new concerns		x		
19.	You take risks & also accept 80 %-solutions (negation)	xv	xv		
20.	You have outbursts of anger	x			

(Source: Own illustration)

Key:

Compulsive	Compulsive/relentless workaholic
Savour	Savouring workaholic
Binge	Binge/bulimic workaholic
Deficit	Attention-deficit workaholic
xv	Allocation validated
xtv	Allocation tendentially validated
x	Allocated

If one compares the criteria with the 2005 study, it can be determined that the points 'flawless quality of work' with 71 %, 'taking on tasks, although you do not have to' with 71 % and 'no taking risks' with 67 % can be identified as observable behaviour of employees. This is followed by 'you are the first to arrive each day and the last to leave' with 29 %.

The remaining points were, at the time, assessed as only marginally identifiable.

With the current study, it can be stated that the identifiable behavioural traits brought forward by the human resources departments in 2005 were clearly substantiated by this study, and that the workaholism type of the 'compulsive/relentless' workaholic could with very high probability be present within companies.

Type savouring workaholic

10 questions were allocated to this type, of which six were validated and one question was tendentially validated. The most important difference between this type and the compulsive/relentless type of workaholism is the point 'work results are not submitted in time, for fear of them being faulty', which was tendentially validated by 41 % of those surveyed. If one considers the points 'you do not work well in a team and have no eye for what is essential' (24 %) and 'Collaboration in the team is inhibited, as you are constantly raising new concerns '(18 %) and assess them as a conglomerate with the validated points, one ends up with seven of 10 questions which can be allocated to this type of workaholism, and allow for the tentative conclusion that there is an according probability that companies have a savouring workaholic among their staff.

This conclusion is slightly substantiated in the individual assessment of the case studies, in which 17 % of the test subjects were identified as not submitting their work results on time, for fear they could be faulty.

In the 2005 study (Meißner 2005, p. 158f.), the conclusion was arrived at, due to the small statistical informative value, that the occurrence of this type as well as the risk potential for companies can be assumed to be minor. A review of the literature has confirmed the inconspicuousness of this type of workaholism in day-to-day business operation. The current survey shows, however, that there is relative probability that this type can be found in companies.

Table 15: Comparison of the behaviours allocated to the types of workaholism with the 2005 study

	Workaholic behavioural characteristics	2017	V 17	C 05	S 05	B 05	D 05
1.	They are (not) interested in the work and in the outcome	6 %			4 %		
2.	An absolutely flawless quality of work is their work requirement	88 %	v	71 %	71 %		
3.	They take on tasks, although they do not have to	88 %	v	71 %			
4.	They (do not) learn from mistakes	18 %		8 %	8 %	8 %	8 %
5.	They do not work well in a team and have no eye for what is essential	24 %		13 %	13 %	13 %	13 %
6.	They take work home	71 %	v	0 %			
7.	They work weekends and while on holiday	71 %	v	0 %	0 %		
8.	They seek new tasks, although not having completed old ones	71 %	v				25 %
9.	They do (not) make creative contributions	29 %			8 %		
10.	Their day-to-day work is characterised by hectic and uncoordinated styles of work	59 %	v			17 %	17 %
11.	Small talk about private matters does not take place, as they are solely fixated on work	59 %	v	4 %			
12.	They are the first to arrive each day and the last to leave	53 %	v	29 %			
13.	They do not tolerate work errors in others	53 %	v	17 %			
14.	They excessively control their colleagues/co-workers, because they do not trust them to be able to complete the tasks independently	53 %	v	0 %			
15.	They are (not) able to delegate tasks	59 %	v	0 %	0 %	0 %	
16.	They are moody	41 %	tv	0 %			
17.	Work results are not submitted in time, for fear of them being faulty	41 %	tv		0 %		
18	Collaboration in the team is inhibited, as they are constantly raising new concerns	18 %			0 %		
19.	They do (not) take risks and also accept 80 %-solutions	82 %	v	67 %	67 %		
20.	They suffer outbursts of anger	18 %		0 %			

(Source: Own illustration)

Key:

V 17	Validation 2017 study
C 05	Compulsive/relentless workaholic, 2005 study
S 05	Savouring workaholic, 2005 study
B 05	Binge/bulimic workaholic, 2005 study
D 05	Attention-deficit workaholic, 2005 study
v	Validation
tv	Allocation tendentially validated

Conclusion:
From a human resources point of view this means an addition to the focus of the investigation: Companies will have to find a way to identify the less obvious forms of the savouring workaholic alongside the compulsive/relentless workaholic.

Binge/bulimic workaholics and attention-deficit workaholics
For these two types of workaholism, just as in the 2005 study, there is no valid statistical evidence in the current survey.

For the binge/bulimic workaholic the point 'your day-to-day work is characterised by hectic and uncoordinated styles of work' (59 %) and 'you are not able to delegate tasks' (59 %) were indeed validated, but there are not enough points to make a clear statement.

For the attention-deficit workaholic the points 'your day-to-day work is characterised by hectic and uncoordinated styles of work' (59 %) and 'you seek new tasks, although not having completed old ones' (71 %) are also validated, but too few in number.

Based on the numbers, it can be assumed that these types of workaholism may also be present in companies, but there is no valid statistical evidence.

In conclusion, it can be stated that the theses regarding these questions can be regarded as tendentially confirmed in the positive: The symptoms, characteristics and the types of workaholism were, based on the study, predominantly confirmed, and the compulsive/relentless type of workaholism clearly stood out. Thus, it has become clear that companies must anticipate that they are with high probability employing a workaholic employee and that they have to consider a high risk potential.

4.2.2 Operational influences on the development or promotion of workaholism

The data analysis in this chapter is to show, to what extent colleagues, management or operational framework conditions may influence the development or promotion of workaholism. For this, the following theses were drawn up:

Thesis 4	Operational influences on the development/promotion of workaholism
Thesis 4.1	*Workaholism is caused by or promoted by operational influences.*
Thesis 4.2	*Management have a decisive influence on the development or promotion of workaholism.*

To investigate these theses, the following question was to clarify to what extent typical fears in regard to work have contributed to the development of workaholism in those surveyed. For this reason, a closer look was taken at the colleagues, the operational framework conditions, and the management.

'Hereafter follows a description of typical fears people have in regard to their work. To what extent have these fears contributed to the development of your workaholism?'

Colleagues (see Figure 6)

The fear of losing the trust of executives and colleagues and that thereby conflicts may develop within the team (47 %), correlates with the statement that fears of the loss of social inclusion within the company, meaning also within the team, exist (41 %) and are seen as points promoting workaholism. The question to pose at this point is whether workaholic employees rather tend to strive for a harmonious work environment, to perhaps be able to live out their workaholism undisturbed or discreetly within the company? This would fit the evaluation of this study, according to which 88 % of those surveyed confirm that they neglect their private environment, meaning family and friends, in favour of work, which constitutes typical workaholic behaviour. Furthermore, additional work caused by the absences of colleagues (47 %) as well as work density and

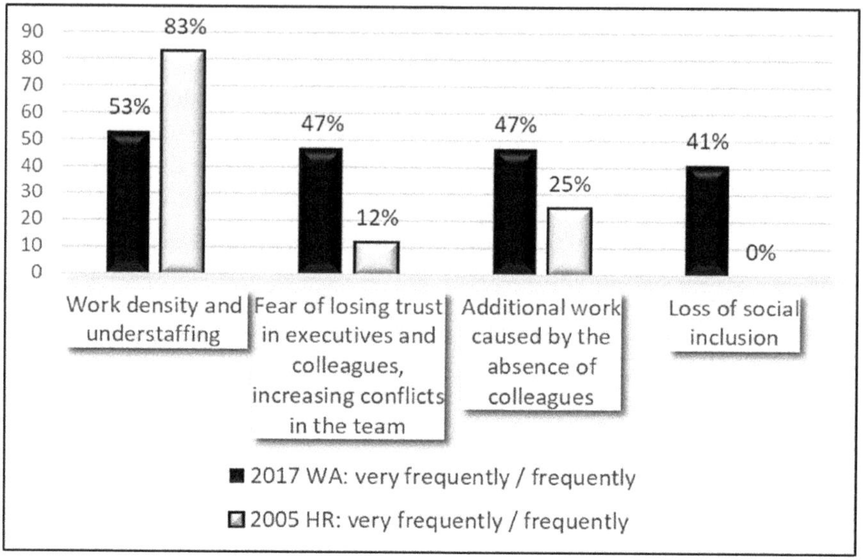

Figure 6: Fears relating to colleagues in comparison with the 2005 study
(Source: Own illustration)

understaffing (53 %) were named as further fears, also having contributed to the development of workaholism. This mirrors a general trend that staff absences and short-staffing often have to be compensated for by the remaining employees, potentially creating a vicious circle, in which the remaining employees become ill through the increased workload or, as hinted at in this study, the situation may positively influence the development of workaholism.

Operational framework conditions (see Figure 7)

This form of corporate culture is also mirrored in the evaluation of the operational framework conditions, where 41 % stated that the cutting of the work budget may lead to a higher work density, insecurity and existential fears, and in turn constitute a corporate policy factor mitigating the development of workaholism. Further to this, generally too much overtime (53 %), the fear of losing employment (53 %) as well as the fear to not be able to withstand the professional pressure (76 %) were named as factors promoting workaholism. This leads to the tentative assumption that increasing market pressure, if passed on to the employees unfiltered, creates an operational framework which may promote workaholism. Unfiltered means that management often does not succeed in

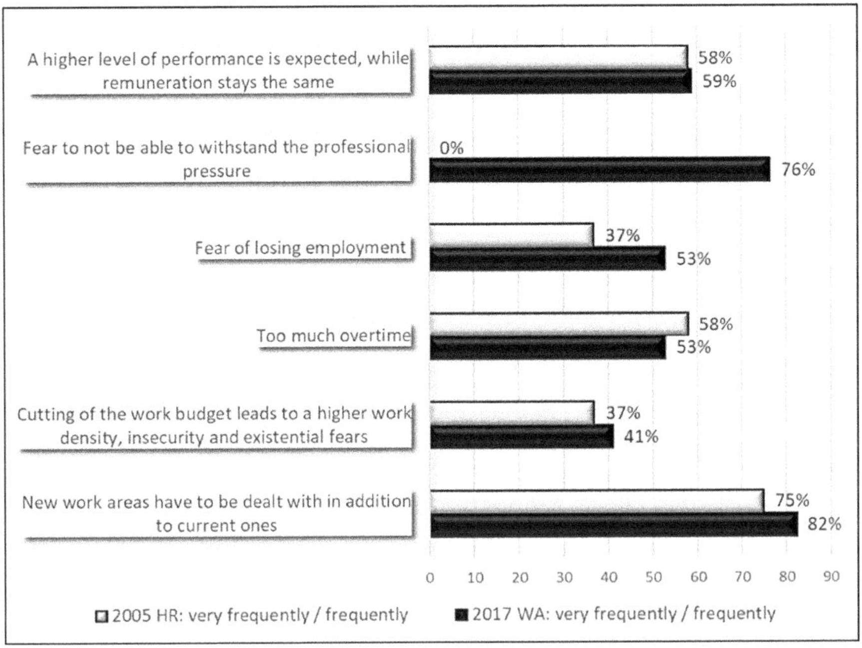

Figure 7: Fears relating to operational framework conditions in comparison with the 2005 study

(Source: Own illustration)

taking away or mitigating their employees' existential fears through open communication and transparency. This is unequivocally a management task that, if not applied, will incite fear within the company.

A further question on the operational framework conditions was whether the working time model promoted living out the workaholism. This is confirmed by 65 % of those surveyed. 54 % of them work under the following working time models: trust-based working hours (24 %), time recording with flexible working time arrangements and flexitime account larger than 40 hours (12 %) as well as time recording with fixed core working time and flexitime account larger than 40 hours (18 %). This confirms the assumption that the freer the working time regulation is within a company, the more undisturbed an employee can indulge in workaholism. The high level of flexibility of employees takes on a special meaning with this.

If one compares the statements of those directly affected with the perspective of the human resources departments from 2005 (see Meißner 2005, p. 178f.), there are obvious parallels. While the human resources departments assessed the high work density and understaffing as occurs very frequently/occurs frequently at 83 %, 53 % of those affected see this as a factor triggering workaholism. There is also a clear agreement on the point 'new work areas have to be dealt with in addition to current ones', which, in 2005, took on a very high significance at 75 %, but was assessed by those affected themselves at an even higher 82 % as a possible trigger of workaholism. Almost equivalent points are the items 'a higher level of performance is expected, while remuneration stays the same', which the human resources departments confirm at 58 % and the test subjects confirm at 59 %, as well as 'too much overtime', which at that time were assessed at 58 % as occurs very frequently/occurs frequently and now have been put at 53 %, and thus definitely have to be taken into account within the spectrum of workaholism triggering factors. The point 'fear of losing employment', as well as 'cutting of the work budget lead to a higher work density, insecurity and existential fears' played a rather minor role in 2005 with 37 % each. The point 'fear to not be able to withstand the professional pressure' was not included in the 2005 survey.

Conclusion:
In this context, it can be stated that the 2005 study clearly recognised the fears of employees regarding operational framework conditions, and that the current study accordingly confirms these fears as possible workaholism triggering factors.

Managers (see Figure 8)
The assessment of the role of managers in the 2005 study, however, stands in contradiction to the results of those surveyed in this study, in which managers are also seen as responsible, as triggering with their management behaviour fears in the employees, which may in turn trigger workaholism. This is illustrated in Figure 8.

The much lower numbers of the 2005 study can probably be explained by the lack of proximity of the human resources department, which seemingly were too far removed from the day-to-day working life in the departments. Indeed, these large discrepancies should encourage human resources departments to think about what they can do to receive realistic assessments from within the departments and to be closer to the employees and management. The risk of misjudgements is obvious here, and should be taken into account in their application of human resources development tools.

It becomes rather strongly apparent in this study the high level of influence managers have on their employees in general, and on the development of workaholism specifically.

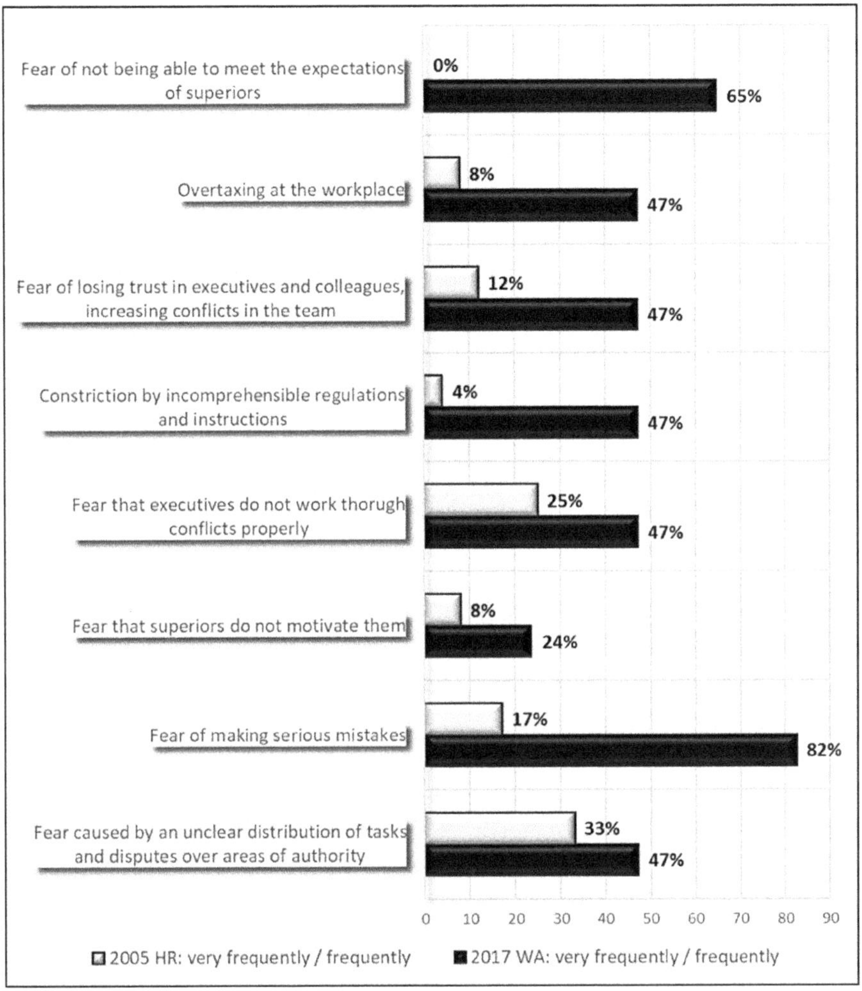

Figure 8: Fears relating to management in comparison with the 2005 study
(Source: Own illustration)

Striking is the point 'fear of making serious mistakes' (82 %), which correlates with the workaholic behaviour 'an absolutely flawless quality of work is their work requirement' (88 %) which are often closely interlinked and are to be regarded as a typical characteristic of the addiction. Added to that is the point 'fear of not being able to meet the expectations of superiors' (65 %). The question has to be asked - what kind of team and management culture superiors create that causes such fears in employees?

24 % of the test subjects stated that they had fears that their superiors were not motivating them, meaning by implication, that they do not properly support them in their work. This statement is complemented by the fact that 47 % feel constricted by incomprehensible regulations and instructions and 47 % experience fear caused by an unclear distribution of tasks and disputes over areas of authority. Also, 47 % of those surveyed expressed the fear that management did not fulfil their role properly and did not work through conflicts. In this context, 47 % confirm that they were afraid that their trust towards executives and colleagues would diminish, and that from that conflict would arise. At total of 47 % of the test subjects felt overtaxed at their workplace. From this it becomes apparent that an untrained manager who does not show clear leadership, and does not look after the needs of the employees, may fuel disorientation and fears that may lead to the development of workaholism in people with addictive personalities.

In summary, it must be stated that the statistical evaluation of the development of workaholism is often situated at midrange around 50 %. It is difficult to draw clear conclusions from this, especially with the low number of test subjects. The theses put forward in this context are therefore not clearly verifiable, but can also not be dismissed. Hence, they should definitely be taken seriously by companies as possible reasons for the development or promotion of workaholism.

Conclusion:
Companies, managers and human resources departments should become more aware of the fact that the practiced corporate policy and managerial behaviour in general may cause fears in employees. Individual expressions may trigger workaholism and specifically even promote its formation. According to this survey, this especially applies to the design of the operational framework conditions. The behaviour of management executives plays a key role in this: On the one hand, managers create the operational framework conditions, and, on the other hand, they actively influence the employees through their own managerial behaviour, and therefore also, the development or promotion of workaholism. This confirms the necessary prioritisation of risk analysis in regard to managers.

4.2.3 Operational consequences of workaholism - self assessment

The following analysis aims to examine how those affected assess the impact of their workaholic behaviour on their working environment. For this purpose, the following thesis was developed:

Thesis 5	*Operational consequences of workaholism were assessed as less negative in the self-assessment of workaholics.*

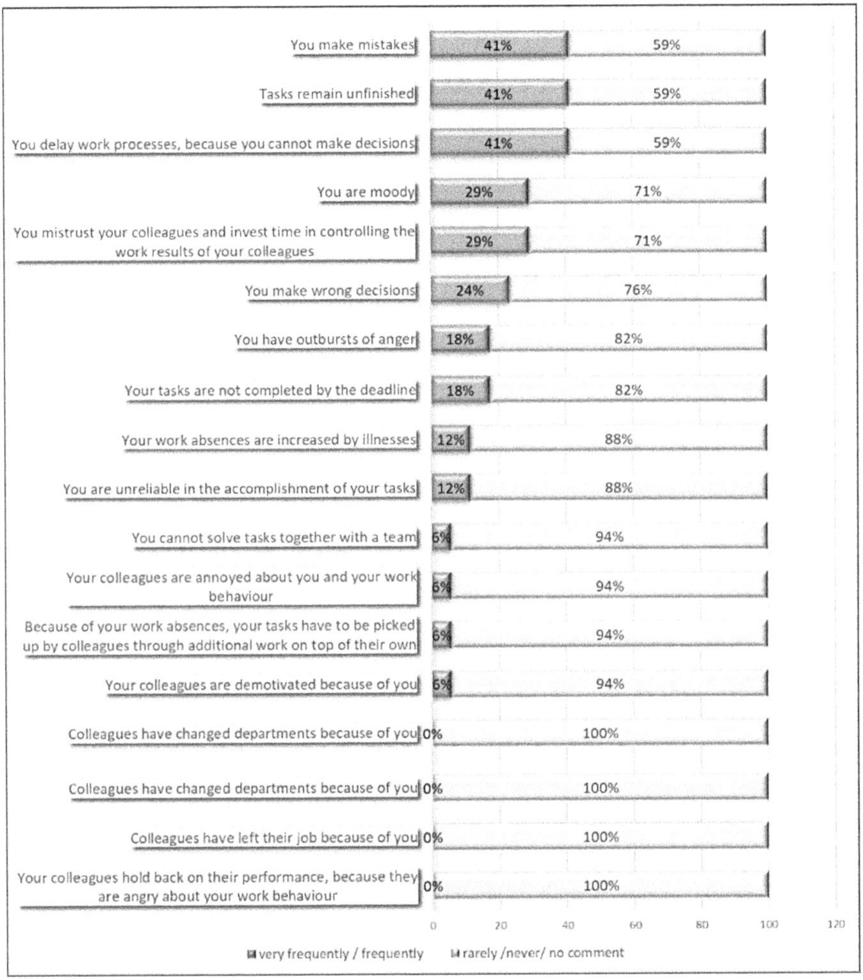

Figure 9: Self-assessment of operational consequences of workaholism in comparison with the 2005 study

(Source: Own illustration)

The equivalent question is:

'How do you assess the operational consequences of your workaholic behaviour?'

Compared to the previous points, this question has another dimension: The previous questions had a descriptive character, which means, those affected described themselves, their fears, their behaviours and symptoms. With this question, the affected person had to think about how their behaviour was affecting third parties or their business environment respectively (see Figure 9). This further dimension can have two effects: on the one hand, it takes courage to admit to oneself that one's own work behaviour may have a negative impact on the company and on colleagues. Generally, people tend to assess themselves more favourably compared to when they were assessed by others. This effect becomes apparent in the point 'your tasks are not completed by the deadline' (18 %), which in the description of behaviour in the point 'work results are not submitted on time for fear of them being faulty' (41 %, Table 13) was assessed as higher.

On the other hand, it is naturally difficult to judge an impact on others, if the latter do not communicate this with those affected. From experience, employees who have handed in their notice do not usually cite the workaholism of a colleague or a management executive as a reason for their leaving. The points 'colleagues have left their job because of you', 'colleagues have changed departments because of you' or 'your colleagues hold back on their performance, because they are angry about your work behaviour' clearly demonstrate this.

The point 'because of your work absences, your tasks have to be picked up by colleagues through additional work on top of their own' (6 %), however, clearly correlates with the assessment of work absences, which were assessed as low in this study.

Interesting are the points 'you make wrong decisions' (24 %) and 'you make mistakes' (41 %), which illustrate that the high demands 'an absolutely flawless quality of work is your work requirement' (88 %, Table 13) cannot be upheld over time, and those affected generally concede this to be true. If one assumes the above whitewash effect to take place, one can expect a much higher hidden number here.

The self-assessment 'you mistrust your colleagues and invest time in controlling the work results of your colleagues' (29 %) also significantly deviates in this point from the behaviour description 'you excessively control you colleagues/co-workers, because you do not trust them to be able to complete the tasks independently', which, at 53 % (Table 13), was also assessed as much higher.

Additionally, this point does not correlate with the statement that those affected at 94 % disagree with the point 'you cannot solve tasks together with a team'. If the team were to be questioned on this matter, a divergent assessment would be rather likely, as it is in human nature to object to excessive control.

The point 'tasks remain unfinished' (41 %) correlates with the behavioural trait 'you seek new tasks, although not having completed old ones' (71 %, Table 13). Here, the consequence that tasks remain unfinished is described more clearly and can be declared a risk factor.

'You delay work processes, because you cannot make decisions' (41 %) is coherent with the behaviour description 'work results are not submitted in time, for fear of them being faulty' (41 %, Table 13). Here, also, a risk potential for deadline delay can be identified.

Inconspicuous, in turn, was the negative impact because of work absences. There were no findings on which consequences the workaholic behaviour had on colleagues and co-workers.

This analysis has shown that the self-assessment of the test subjects in regard to the impact of their addiction on their work deviates from the overall assessment of this study. This deviation can probably be explained by the phenomenon that it is easier for people to describe themselves and the characteristics of their illness than to reflect on how this could impact on others. The thesis was thus confirmed by the analysis.

Conclusion:
The evaluation specifically resulted in the identification of the following economic and human resources risks:

Consequences	**Risk**
Delay of work processes	Peer to peer pressure, see Chapters 3.3. and 3.4.
Unfinished tasks	Motivation risk, see Chapters 3.3. and 3.4.
Deadline delays	See Chapters 3.3. and 3.4
Control of colleagues	Bottleneck risk, resignation risk, see Chapters 3.3. and 3.4
Mistakes	See Chapters 3.3. and 3.4
Wrong decisions	See Chapters 3.3. and 3.4

These points are generally all irregularities that should be able to be identified by management or by colleagues. This has led to the discovery of further indications which companies might use to detect workaholic employees.

It is to be recorded that workaholic behaviours have a negative impact on companies and are an economic and a human resources risk.

4.2.4 Summary and conclusion of the empirical research outcomes

Thesis 1	*Workaholism affects people irrespective of gender and age.*

The study has illustrated that the outbreak of this illness is not dependent on gender. This had also been confirmed in previous studies.

Thesis 2	*Workaholism primarily affects people with aca-demic degrees and is specifically a managerial disease.*

It could be shown that workaholism is obviously more prevalent among people with an academic degree. If one compares the studies by Vicario and Voigt, this tendency can be confirmed. However, it could not be unambiguously confirmed or denied that workaholism primarily affected management executives and was therefore rather a managerial disease.

Thesis 3	Indication of workaholism.
Thesis 3.1	*The indications for workaholism in the form of characteristics, symptoms and types of workaholism, identified by psychologists and consultants, have been confirmed by the test subjects.*
These 3.2	*Workaholics neglect their health.*
These 3.3	*Workaholics have a higher number of work absences.*

The thesis that workaholics neglect their health can, after this study, be assumed to be most likely true, and can be confirmed. However, it could not be detected that workaholics, at the same time, have a high number of work absences. Here, rather the opposite became apparent. The test subjects had, on average, considerably less time off work.

Thesis 3.4	*The attendance of the support group Workaholics Anonymous has a positive effect on the severity of the illness.*

The analysis of the symptoms seems to affirm that the test subjects in this study, as participants in Workaholics Anonymous meetings, showed a tendency towards less serious illnesses. It can be deduced from this how important and prophylactic the work of Workaholics Anonymous is. This conclusion is generally validated by the data of the cumulative study. At this point, this Thesis seems to have been confirmed.

Thesis 3.5	*The properties of the compulsive/relentless type of workaholism are more prevalent than those of the remaining types.*

The symptoms, characteristics and the types of workaholism were predominantly confirmed by the subjects of this study and the compulsive/relentless type of workaholism has emerged clearly. Thus, it has become apparent that companies are extremely likely to have workaholics among their employees and that a corresponding risk potential has to be factored in.

Thesis 4	Operational influences on the development and promotion of workaholism.
Thesis 4.1	*Workaholism is caused by or promoted by operational influences.*
Thesis 4.2	*Management have a decisive influence on the de-velopment or promotion of workaholism.*

The statistical evaluation of these theses often is situated more or less at midrange around 50 %. To draw unambiguous conclusions from this is difficult, especially given the low number of test subjects. The theses put forward in this context are therefore not clearly verifiable, but can also not be dismissed. Hence, the operational influences on the workaholism issue should definitely be taken into account and observed. Nonetheless, the central significance of the role of managers for the development or promotion of workaholism cannot be denied, and therefore carries a high corporate and human responsibility in regard to workaholism.

Thesis 5	*Operational consequences of workaholism were assessed as less negative in the self-assessment of workaholics.*

The analysis has shown that the self-assessment of the test subjects in relation to the impact of their addiction on their work deviates from the overall assessment of this study. This deviation may likely be explained by the phenomenon that it is easier for people to describe themselves and the characteristics of their illness than to reflect on how it could impact other people. Nonetheless, it is possible to identify clear economic and human resources risks, such as delay of work processes, unfinished tasks, deadline delays, control over colleagues, mistakes, wrong decisions.

The evaluation of the entire empirical study has shown that workaholism, from a human resources point of view, is a complex conglomerate of individual workaholic behaviours, operational influences and human resources risks. Specifically, this complexity, and the mutual interactive structure of companies and workaholics, make it clear that for the identification of this illness a structured system of instruments is required, which must be interactively connected and linked up with each other. For the application of this system, a professional analytical instrument is required in order to proceed in an economic and objective oriented manner. This can happen in the form of human resources risk management, which constitutes a sound starting point for all operational and human resources matters, and will be exemplarily discussed in Chapter 6. For a deeper look into the significance of human resources risks through workaholism, a corresponding risk analysis will be carried out in the following chapter with the results of the current study.

5 Risk analysis on the basis of research results

The reasons why it makes economic sense to deal with workaholism, and to integrate it with the analysis for human resources risks, is demonstrated in the following practical example. The example at hand concerns only a small partial aspect, namely the survey of costs measurable in the short term. Clearly more significant effects, such as loss of benefit, process control, or loss of expertise may be given as well. Table 16 demonstrates, therefore, which direct and indirect costs could be traced back to a workaholic superior of the type 'compulsive/relentless worker':[25] Three external recruitments, one in-house transfer, one in-house transfer during the trial period, staff appraisals with employees, who could not live up to the requirements of their superior, as well as the work absences of the superior. This has resulted in a human resources value added loss in the amount of approximately € 217,000 and approximately 306 days (approximately 1.4 full-time capacity). This sum, but specifically the high level of unproductive time, can be identified as an absolute existential threat for smaller companies, especially when the person in question is a key player.

Table 16: Example of a total cost scenario caused by a workaholic superior

	Time volumes in hours per occurrence	EUR per occurrence	Factor	Total time in hours	EUR total
Cost of an internal transfer	197	19.664	1	197	19.664
Cost of an internal transfer during the probationary period	346	19.377	1	346	19.377
3 external recruitments	217	44.210	3	651	132.630
Conversations with employees	57	5.520	1	57	5.520
Absenteeism of the executive	1.195	39.285	1	1.195	39.285
Total				**2.446**	**216.475**

(Source: Meißner 2005, p. 129: Own illustration, costs in accordance with the inflation rate of the German Federal Statistical Office from 2005 to 2017 inflated by 18 %.[26]

This example clearly demonstrates, how important it is from a human resources perspective to identify workaholism early, in order to help those

25 A detailed calculation of the costs and time volumes can be found in Meißner's 2005 study, Chapter 4.3.

26 German Federal Statistical Office, 04/2017, p. 20–23, https://www.destatis.de/DE/Publikationen/Thematisch/Preise/Verbraucherpreise/VerbraucherpreisindexLangeReihenPDF_5611103.pdf.)

affected in a targeted fashion and to stave off monetary as well as non-material damage from businesses.

This chapter will see a specific risk analysis using the data and findings from the empirical study, aiming to show more clearly the risk potential that exists for businesses. More specifically, workaholic behaviour traits, symptoms of workaholism as well as operational influences on the development or promotion of workaholism, will undergo a risk assessment.

The risk assessment will be based on the following four categories:

- High degree of spread and high degree of impact = high risk potential as well as a strong indication for the potential presence of workaholism indications or for potential addiction triggering/addiction promoting operational influences respectively
- High degree of spread and low degree of impact = medium risk potential as well as a medium indication for the potential presence of workaholism indications or for potential addiction triggering/addiction promoting operational influences respectively
- Low degree of spread and high degree of impact = medium risk potential as well as a medium indication for the potential presence of workaholism indications or for potential addiction triggering/addiction promoting operational influences respectively
- Low degree of spread and low degree of impact = low risk potential as well as a weak indication for the potential presence of workaholism indicators or for potential addiction triggering/addiction promoting operational influences respectively.

5.1 Risk analysis of workaholic behaviour traits

In the following analysis, traits of workaholic behaviour are divided into 'visible behaviours' (white boxes) and 'invisible behaviours' (grey boxes).

In the risk assessment of the behaviour traits, the probability of occurrence was valued at the degree of spread from the survey and the expectation of damage at the degree of impact. The degree of impact stands for the assessment of the extent to which a certain workaholic behaviour may have an effect on the fulfilment of the work.

If one look at the typical behaviours of workaholics in Figure 10 in a risk portfolio, it becomes clear that 25 % of the behaviour traits were validated and pose a high risk potential for businesses. 40 % of the criteria, in addition, pose a medium risk potential.

The criteria with the highest risk potential are mainly *easily recognisable behaviours*, which, moreover, may have an immediate influence on the quality of the work outcomes and the productivity:

The absolutely flawless quality of work as well as the lacking in acceptance of 80 % solutions may develop into an infinite loop, which would implicate unjustified schedule delays, without sustainably improving the quality of the work results. The productivity of the co-workers and of the team will be extremely reduced by this. This also applies to working behaviour, which involves looking for new tasks, although the old ones have not yet been completed. This also comes with a high risk that deadlines are delayed, and that within the work processes, colleagues involved will not be able to complete their own tasks. The conflicts arising from this were presented in detail in Chapter 2. Hectic and uncoordinated styles of work also have a direct influence on the quality of work and on the error rate.

The criteria 'working at the weekend/on holiday/at home', 'are the first to arrive each day and the last to leave' are to be regarded as working time criteria, to be assessed as a medium risk potential, because, although it is a behaviour that is immediately visible, it may only have an indirect or delayed negative effect on productivity and the quality of work. This becomes the case, as soon as the person affected has lost control over his working behaviour and reacts in a compulsive fashion. Then the risk potential constantly increases. Otherwise, these points can per se be allocated to people who work a lot, but for whom these behaviours do not initially necessarily have a negative effect.

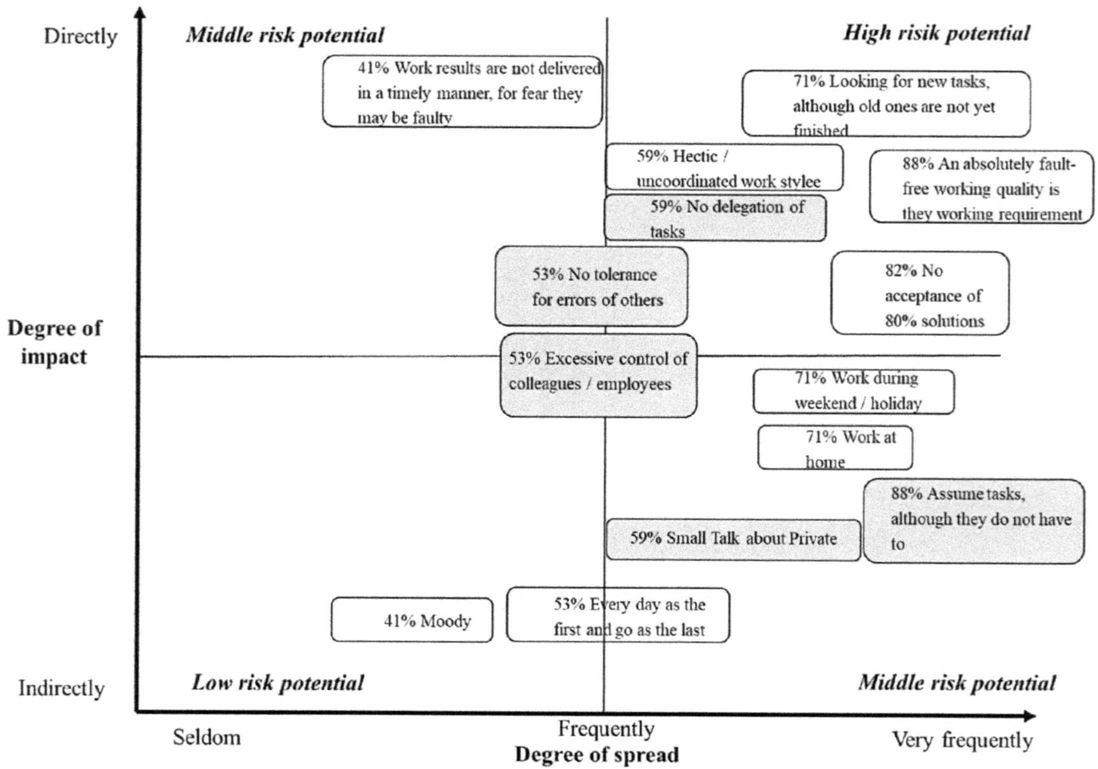

Figure 10: Risk portfolio behaviour traits of workaholics
(Source: Own illustration)

The remaining *invisible criteria* can have an effect on work quality and productivity, but have the tendency to only reveal their negative impact after some time, and are not immediately noticed by third parties. These rather are work process criteria that must be observed over a longer period.

Conclusion:
In this study, workaholic behaviour traits have emerged which should be observable to third parties. This leads to the conclusion that it is possible for companies to identify workaholic behaviours and to approach them from a risk management point of view in line with their economic strategy and, at the same time, meet their duty of care towards those affected.

5.2 Risk analysis of workaholism symptoms

To develop an approach for companies, to make the symptoms of workaholism identifiable for third parties, the illnesses pertaining to the addiction were generally classified into 'visible' and 'invisible' symptoms. In Figure 11, the visible workaholic symptoms are displayed in white boxes, and the invisible symptoms in grey boxes. Invisible illnesses only become transparent for companies when those affected declare themselves or inform colleagues or superiors of their illness. Thus, it is primarily those symptoms visible to the outside that can be detected and assessed by third parties through careful observation and empathy, without being reliant on the assistance of those affected themselves. Table 17 shows the classification, together with the results of the survey. In Figure 11 it becomes clear that on the basis of the analysis, the visible behavioural symptoms clearly emerge and thereby prove that companies can identify behavioural workaholic symptoms.

Table 17: 'Visible'/'invisible' data analysis of symptoms

Externally visible physical symptoms	**Externally invisible physical symptoms**
• 24% Allergies • 18% Shortness of breath (high blood pressure) • 18% Nervous tics • 35% Dizziness • Trembling hands	• 41% Headache • 76% Permanent exhaustion • 53% Digestive problems • 24% Stomach pain • 6% Ulceration • 29% Stinging in the chest (heart disease) • 41% Back pain • 41% Sudden hearing loss
Externally visible behavioural symptoms	**Externally invisible behavioural symptoms**
• 76% Mood swings (euphoria / depression, mental illnesses) • 76% Concentration problems • 29% Outbursts of anger • 94% Unrest • 71% Forgetfulness • 65% Hyperactivity • 76% Irritability and impatience	• 88% Tension • 82% Sleep disorders • Inability to relax • Boredom

(Source: Own illustration; the points without numerical value have not been surveyed.)

In the risk assessment of the symptoms, the probability of occurrence was valued at the degree of spread from the survey and the expectation of damage at the degree of impact. The degree of impact stands for the assessment of the extent to which a certain illness may have an effect on the fulfilment of the work. Allergies, for example, have a relatively low degree of spread according to the survey, and generally speaking hamper the work productivity to a lesser extent. Permanent exhaustion and sleep disorders, on the other hand, have a stronger impact, as overtired employees perform less well. Their irritability and impatience can also negatively impact the mood within the team and thus impair team results.

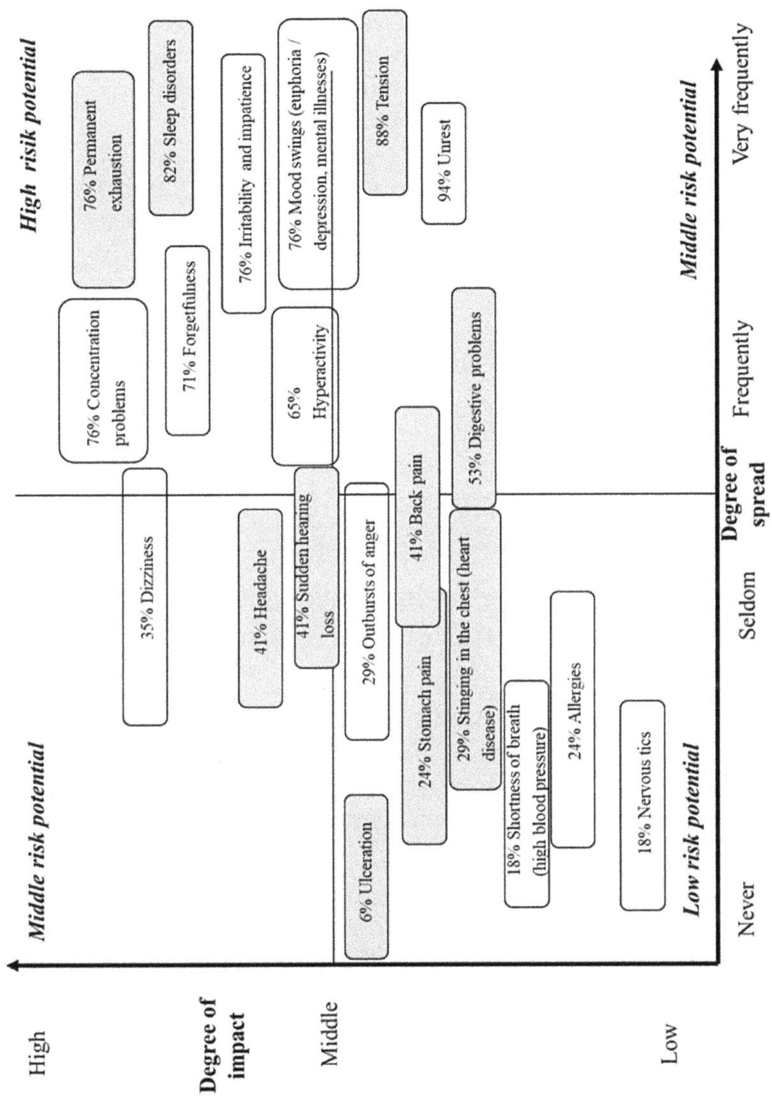

Figure 11: Risk portfolio symptoms of workaholism
(Source: Own illustration)

If one applies the survey results to a risk portfolio, it becomes evident that the symptoms visible to the outside also imply the highest risk potential for companies. If one looks at the illnesses of the invisible symptoms, one can tendentially assume that these illnesses occur more or less in intervals, which, at the time of occurrence (example: headache), distract the employee from work and carry the risk of mistakes being made or loss of quality. When the pain subsides, the above risk falls again. With the visible symptoms, one tends to not expect an occurrence in intervals, but rather an increasingly permanent state. These criteria imply a high risk potential in regard to the emergence of mistakes and quality losses in work results. Deadline delays and a decreasing productivity on the part of the affected party are to be expected.

Conclusion:
33 % of the symptoms pose a high risk potential for companies, whereby even 24 % of which are visible to the outside. A total of 62 % of workaholism symptoms can be assigned a medium to high risk potential. The numbers indicate a clear necessity for a detailed illness analysis within the company in the form of, for example, quantitative and qualitative assessment of work absences or feedback from superiors and the team, in order to verify the risks and to initiate the respective action measures for the reduction of said risks.

5.3 Risk analysis of operational influences on the development or promotion of workaholism

The following analysis is to illustrate the findings on the influences of colleagues and operational framework conditions, as well as of management in the development or promotion of workaholism in a risk portfolio.

In Figure 12, the influences of management are displayed in white boxes, the influences of operation framework conditions in grey boxes, and the influence of colleagues in shaded boxes.

In the risk assessment of the influencing characteristics, the probability of occurrence was valued at the degree of spread from the survey and the expectation of damage at the degree of impact. The degree of impact stands for the assessment of the extent to which an influencing characteristic may have an effect on the fulfilment of the work.

The evaluation of the degree of impact was determined in terms of the extent to which the points listed would have an effect on companies, directly and promptly (=higher risk) or indirectly and over a period of time (=lower risk).

Against this background, the risk potential relating to colleagues appears in the middle spectrum of the portfolio and, thus, is also given an equivalent medium risk priority. The point 'High work density and understaffing' is worth mentioning

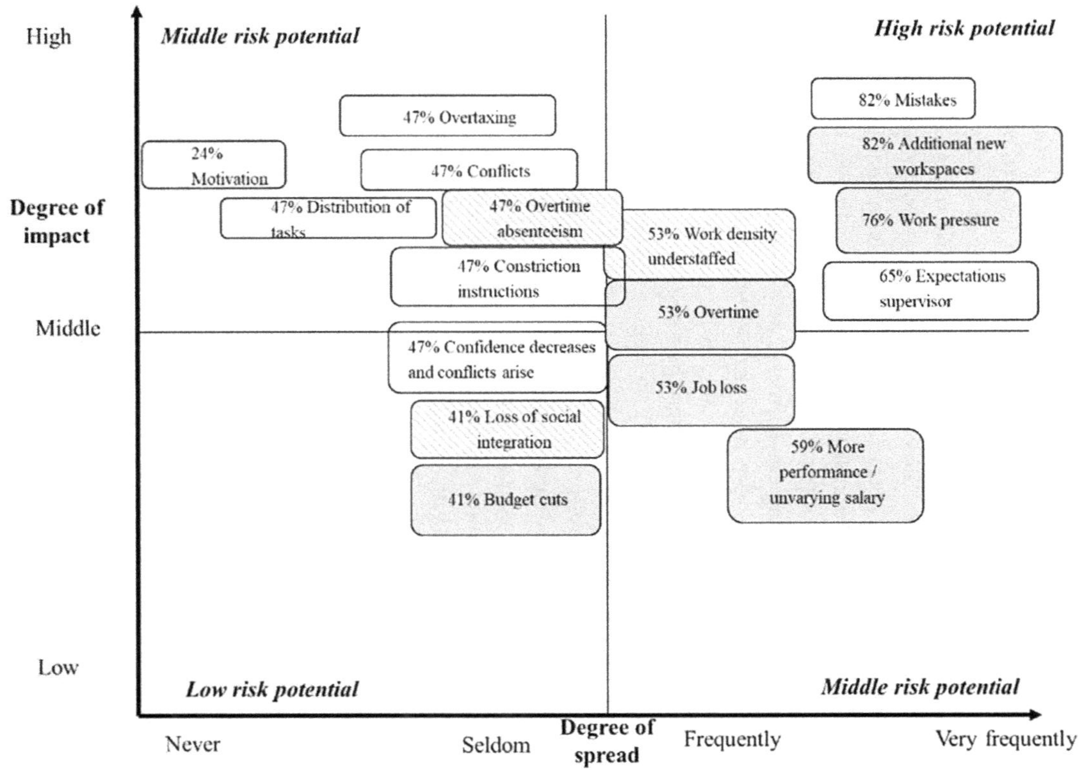

Figure 12: Risk portfolio of operational influences on the development/promotion of workaholism
(Source: Own illustration)

at this point, as these work conditions may have a direct impact on the quality of work results and thereby pose an economic risk. Moreover, this will lead to a human resources risk, if employees are continuously exposed to this work situation. Work absences, demotivation or unwanted resignations may follow.

More noteworthy are the operational framework conditions, of which, after all, 50 % are located in a high-risk area and which, therefore, have to be assigned a higher significance. The points 'new work areas have to be dealt with in addition to current ones', 'fear to not be able to withstand the professional pressure' as well as 'too much overtime' can have a direct and prompt effect on the quality of the work results, and lead to limited performance levels. This is an unacceptable economic risk for companies. For that reason, a higher degree of impact was assumed here. The points 'a higher level of performance is expected, while remuneration stays the same', 'the fear of losing employment', as well as 'cutting of the work budget lead to a higher work density, insecurity and existential fears' are in this context assessed lower on the impact scale, as they more likely indirectly and over the long term reveal their manifestation and their impact.

Very significant in the risk portfolio is the degree of impact of management behaviour. Apart from one exception, all points surveyed have a direct and prompt impact on the work results and the work behaviour of employees. These employees are directly impacted in their ability to work and may fall into a work situation which may promote workaholism. This becomes especially evident in the points 'fear of making serious mistakes' as well as 'fear of not being able to meet the expectations of superiors', which, on the basis of their high degree of spread, have to be assigned to the category of 'high risk potential'.

The risk portfolio thus clearly shows the special responsibility of management executives for all employees within the company in general, and their influence potential on the development and promotion of workaholism in companies in particular.

Conclusion:
The risk portfolio of the operational influences on the development or promotion of workaholism again demonstrated the special responsibility of management, which reinforces the recommendation to look urgently at the management level of a company, when planning the priorities for a risk analysis.

This chapter has shown that workaholic behaviours and illnesses pose a significant risk potential for companies. It took the economic and human resources risks from Chapter 3 and substantiated them through the results of the study in the described risk portfolio analysis. Ways to identify workaholism traits for third parties, as well as the special role that managers hold in this, have clearly emerged.

6 Actions guidelines

In this chapter, the focus is on the application of the instruments of risk analysis in regard to workaholism, as well as on supporting measures helping management identify issues of workaholism.[27] From that, recommendations for action are derived, supported by practical action guidelines.

6.1 Possibilities for risk analysis of workaholism in companies

The identification of workaholic employees is difficult from the point of view of the company, but not impossible. A fundamental prerequisite is the recognition of workaholism as an illness, and as an economic risk with serious consequences on the working environment, the operational processes, the quality of work and the work outcomes respectively. This constitutes a widening of perspective, which does not *necessarily* require innovation in existing human resources processes and instruments, but, at the most, the adjustment of existing instruments in their relation to workaholism criteria, or a newly defined analytical focus against the background of workaholism.

The following instruments, for example, can be used in risk analysis:[28]

- Employee surveys
- Personnel information talk
- Work-Ability-Index
- Work Addiction Risk Test
- Analysis of work absences
- Fluctuation analyses

These instruments can, without great effort, be checked for workaholism characteristics, or adjusted respectively, and will be illustrated in the following chapters.

27 The elaborations are an addition to the recommendations given by the author of this study in her 2005 study, in which the focus lay on the employment legislation evaluation and the presentation of adequate human resources instruments in regard to workaholism.

28 For detailed information on the instruments' employee surveys, personnel information talk, work absences and fluctuation analysis, as well as their adjustment towards workaholism traits, please see Meißner's 2005 study.

6.1.1 Employee surveys and personnel information talk

a) Employee surveys

For the basic analysis, the instruments employee surveys and personnel information talk, in which all employees are included, can be used.

An employee survey has the advantage that comprehensive questions on workaholism traits can be directly incorporated and evaluated. Employee surveys are usually conducted along a specific line of questions that a company would like to examine. The scope of the questions often orients itself along the degree of necessity for change. If a company faces the challenge of a comprehensive change management process, a wide range of topics is addressed in the survey. If it involves a continuous process of change, individual topics are often scrutinised and jointly processed.

Depending on the orientation of the employee survey, workaholism criteria may be added, as the following examples show:

- Focus employee survey 'work environment and work organisation': supplemented by workaholism topics from Chapter 4.2.2. operational influences, working hours model, overtime, work behaviour (for example holiday, weekend).
- Focus employee survey 'health management': supplemented by symptoms/illnesses of workaholism from Chapter 4.2.1.
- Focus employee survey 'management culture': supplemented by workaholism topics from Chapter 4.2.2. 'operational influences'.

By choosing this approach, companies can conduct a comprehensive analysis of workaholism criteria and carry out a corresponding risk assessment. The disadvantage of an employee survey is the high expenditure of time and cost. A professional survey is normally carried out and evaluated by trained employees or by external consultants. This is followed up by recommendations for action, and projects for the implementation of the recommendations.

b) Personnel information talk

The personnel information talk is a pragmatic, cost-effective and efficient human resources instrument, requiring little time or work effort, to implement a risk identification for workaholism. Figure 13 describes the structure of this instrument. It takes place once a year between departmental management and human resources management. At the beginning of the conversation stands a general information exchange between the department and human resources management, to bring to mind the respective current situation, which has the potential of influencing the further course of the discussion. If one department, for example, has been strongly affected by staff cutbacks, the focus of the discussion is a different one from when the department has had to add staff. This is followed by quantitative/operative human resources planning. The focus of the discussion is the analysis of qualitative strengths and weaknesses for all employees of the company, which can be used as the basis for a structured human resources development measure as well as for a risk analysis. Depending on the practised corporate culture in regard to issues of health promotion or the handling of human capital, this instrument may be used by human resources management in a proactive or restrained fashion for the examination of workaholic behaviour. In a proactive approach, direct questions as to workaholic behaviours would be asked in discussion about individual employees. In a restrained approach, the human resources representatives would conduct an indirect risk identification for workaholism, in which they will restrict themselves to general issues of work behaviour and indications of workaholism, without explicitly naming them. With reservations expected from departments, the restrained approach seems to be better suited. A prerequisite for this form of inquiry is trained discussion facilitators, usually human resources representatives, who have extensively dealt with the topic of workaholism and are able to identify and alert others to workaholism traits.

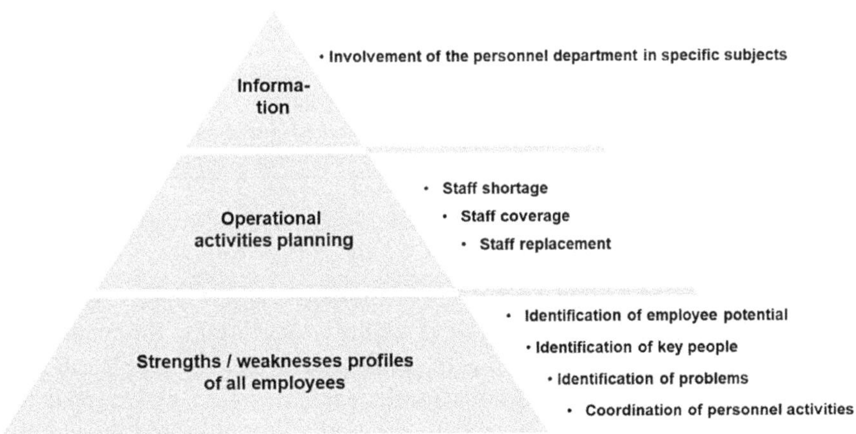

Figure 13: Personnel information talk
(Source: Own illustration)

Consequently, general risk characteristics regarding employee potential, people in key roles, or employees for whom action is required, can be entered into the qualitative approach. In addition, for example, questions from Table 18 on workaholism criteria can be implicated.

6.1.2 Work-Ability-Index and Work Addiction Risk Test

a) Work-Ability-Index

Of pivotal importance for the success of a company is the knowledge which employees will be needed in future, how to recruit them and/or retain them for the company and how to develop them as well as how to motivate them to provide an above average level of commitment. Here, the effects of demographic change on companies has moved the topic of sustainable preservation of work ability of the employees into the central focus of human resources. Ilmarinen has, in this context, developed the 'house of work ability' (see Figure 14), in which the factors influencing work capabilities are represented in the form of a house.

Table 18: Questions for the determination of workaholism criteria

Risk	Reasons
Bottleneck risk:	Questions on *absences* and looking for reasons for absences
Motivation risk:	Questions on the reasons for d*emotivation* (colleagues, work task, suspicious work behaviour)
Adjustment risk:	*Employee attends seminars without success*: looking for reasons, by, for example questioning the work behaviour
Resignation risk:	*Employee is in danger of leaving*: looking for reasons for the departure (working environment, lack of development, colleagues)

(Source: Own illustration)

Ilmarinen emphasises that all levels of the house are of equal importance for the sustainable preservation of work ability in employees. The foundation of the house is health and the ability to perform. Only healthy people can fully deploy their performance ability and contribute it to the company. On top of the foundations lie the competences as well as the values, attitudes and the motivation of employees. The work task and environment, as well as the behaviour of management, complete the description of the prerequisites for sustainable work ability. If one aspect from the respective levels is impaired, the balance is upset,

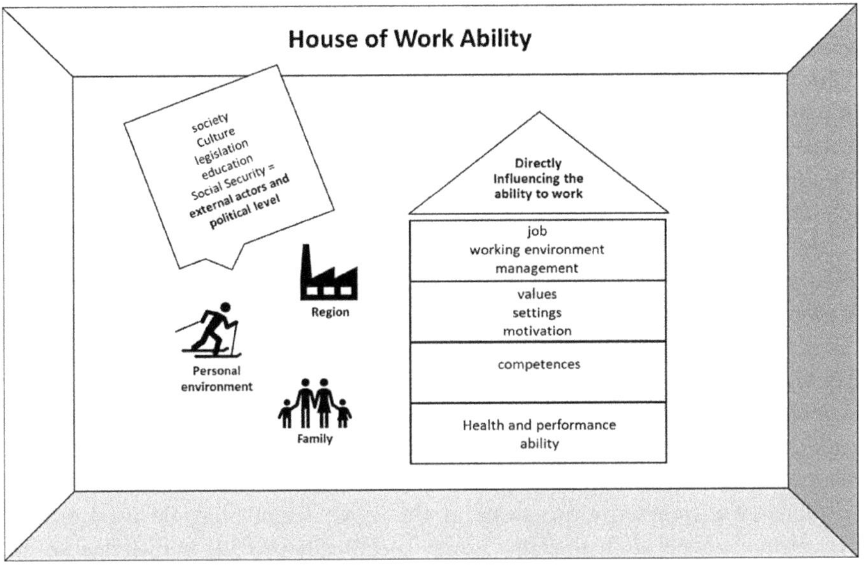

Figure 14: House of Work Ability according to Ilmarinen
(Source: Own illustration, following Temple/Ilmarinen 2013, p. 41)

and work ability is reduced or negatively influenced. What is new to companies are the statements which refer to the way in which the family, the personal environment, the regional environment, and external players/political levels have indirect influence on work ability. For companies, this means a widening of perspectives, and raises the question to what extent also family problems influence work ability, and which measures employers can offer to support their employees through private problems as well.

If one analyses the house of work ability from a workaholism perspective, the levels 'work, work environment and management' as well as 'health and ability to perform' appear in particular focus. These topics were the focus of this study and were examined in Chapter 4 accordingly.

The sustainable preservation of work ability should be the subject matter of a proactive health management which also proactively addresses the topic of workaholism. To determine the current work ability of employees, the Work-Ability-Index (WAI) is used. This will be described hereafter, and is also suitable as an instrument of analysis for the risk assessment of workaholism criteria.

The WAI was developed by Ilmarinen and Tuomi as a result of a project with ageing employees in the Finnish municipal services, and is a measuring instrument for the representation of the indication of current work ability of people in paid employment. It analyses how far people are able to manage their work in the light of work requirements, their personal health and mental resources. The index supplies a measured value for the current proportion of operational requirements and individual or collective performance ability. High values equate a balanced ratio: low values signify an imbalance between both values. In addition, it serves as an early warning indicator of the potential early retirement of employees from employment, or of a looming inability to work (see Temple/ Ilmarinen 2013, p. 117). The University of Wuppertal has made WAI available free for employees and businesses.[29] This gives companies a pragmatic instrument of analysis, to gather a first impression of the work ability of their employees and, building on that, the ability to develop and implement the respective measures relating to the house of work ability.

Table 19 displays the questions of the WAI, which may be used as risk indicators for workaholism traits. It may specifically provide knowledge on the impairment of work ability in connection with possible negative operational influences as well as problems on the interpersonal level. From this, indicators for the development or promotion of workaholism can be deduced. The illnesses listed can be compared with the symptoms of workaholism and assigned to the respective stages.

The WAI-questionnaire[30] clearly shows that it not only displays pragmatically an actual state from which measures can be deduced regarding business health management, but that it is also well suited to conduct an initial analysis for the collection of workaholism characteristics and possible influences on the development or promotion of workaholism in companies, and then from that arrive at a risk assessment.

The advantage of this instrument of analysis lies in its discreet application. Human resources management can evaluate the WAI, without having to communicate publicly that they are also shedding light on the topic of workaholism. This approach proves useful to companies who take a rather restrained approach to workaholism and in which it is not openly discussed.

29 WAI: http://www.arbeitsfaehigkeit.uni-wuppertal.de/index.php?der-wai.

30 http://www.arbeitsfaehigkeit.uni-wuppertal.de/index.php?WAI-Online.

Table 19: Comparison WAI-Questionnaire characteristics of workaholism

WAI Questionnaire	Traits of workaholism
Work ability in relation to work requirements	*Indication of the influences on the development of workaholism.*
How do you assess your current ability to work in relation to the physical work requirements?	Indication of operational influences as to work organisation, colleagues, management. Comparison with the types of illnesses.
How do you assess your current ability to work in relation to the psychological work requirements?	Disturbances in the inter-personal domain/ overtaxed. Comparison with the types of illnesses.
On the following list, tick your illnesses and injuries.	*Stages of workaholism*
Injuries caused by accidents	
Illnesses of the musculoskeletal system	Middle stage
Cardiovascular diseases	Final stage
Respiratory diseases	
Psychological illnesses	Final stage
Neurological & sensory diseases	
Illnesses of the digestive system	Early stage
Venereal diseases and urinary tract diseases	
Dermatological illnesses	
Tumours	
Hormonal and metabolic diseases	
Blood disorders	
Birth defects	
Other illnesses or diseases?	
Estimated restriction to work performance due to illnesses	*Indication for risk evaluation: The higher the value the higher the risk for bottlenecks.*
Sickness rate over the last year: For how many whole days have you been absent from work in the last 12 months due to health issues (illness/accident)?	*Indication for risk evaluation: The higher the number of days absent the higher the risk for bottlenecks.*

(Source: Own illustration)

b) Work Addiction Risk Test

A proactive health management with a transparent brief can also actively perform a workaholism analysis for the company. For this, they may use Robinson's Work Addiction Risk Test (WART) (see Table 20), which shows up workaholism,

Table 20: Work Addiction Risk Test (WART)

1. I prefer to do most things myself rather than ask for help.
2. I get very impatient when I have to wait for someone or when something takes too long.
3. I seem to be in a hurry, racing against the clock.
4. I get irritated when I am interrupted while in the middle of something.
5. I stay busy and keep many irons in the fire.
6. I engage in two or three activities at once, such as eating lunch, checking my email, and talking on my cell phone.
7. I overcommit myself by biting off more than I can chew.
8. I feel guilty when I am not working on a project.
9. It is important that I see the concrete results of my work.
10. I am more interested in the final outcome of my work than in the process.
11. Things don't move fast enough or get done fast enough at work to suit me.
12. I lose my temper when things don't go my way or work out to suit me.
13. I ask the same question over and over again, without realising it, after I've already been given the answer.
14. I work in my head thinking about future projects while tuning out the here and now.
15. I continue working after my co-workers have called it quits.
16. I get angry when people don't meet my standards of perfection on the job.
17. I get upset when I am not in control at work.
18. I tend to put myself under pressure from self-imposed work deadlines.
19. It is hard for me to relax when I'm not working.
20. I spend more time working than socialising with friends or enjoying hobbies or leisure activities.
21. I dive into projects to get a head start before plans are finalised.
22. I get upset with myself for making even the smallest mistake.
23. I put more thought, time, and energy into work than into relationships with loved ones and friends.
24. I forget, ignore or minimise celebrations such as birthdays, reunions, anniversaries or holidays.
25. I make important job decisions before getting all the facts and thinking them through.

(Source: Robinson 2014, p. 23.)

tendencies towards workaholism or merely hard work on the basis of work habits (see Robinson 2000, p. 62 ff., see Robinson 2014, p. 23; Table 23). The statements listed are assessed as '1 = is never the case, 2 = is sometimes the case, 3 = is often the case, 4 = is always the case'. The number which best represents the work habit is written in front of the respective statement. At the end, all numbers are added up. The highest possible result is 100, the lowest 25. The higher the value, the higher the probability, according to Robinson, that someone is a workaholic. The evaluation of the extent of workaholism divides the results into the following groups:

- 67–100 points: suspicion, that full-fledged workaholism is present bearing high health risks
- 57–66 points: suspicion that moderate workaholism is present with good prospects for healing
- 25–56 points: no workaholism; it is probable that the person just works hard

The actions to be taken are naturally strongly dependent on the results. The more employees that are found in the upper third region, meaning that there is suspicion of full-fledged workaholism with a high health risk, the more intensely and more actively activities have to be initiated to minimise the operational risks again and to help those affected. Operational health management has a significant importance here, as comprehensive analyses of operational framework conditions, practised management behaviour and corporate culture in general, as well as the consideration of the situation of individual employees, must follow.

The company-wide application of this instrument constitutes a pure form of workaholism analysis and is to be recommended as such to proactively address this topic.

6.1.3 Analysis of work absences and fluctuation, assessing management executives and employees

a) Analysis of work absences

The risk analysis of work absences within human resources risk management can occur as a preventative method of an early warning system for work absences, as well as a reactive method of illness analysis in the form of check-up interviews.

The structural analysis (following Nieder 1999, p. 137 ff.) constitutes an early warning system with work absence numbers, which deals with the influenceable fraction of absences (motivation-related absences as well as in-house health promotion programmes). The focus is on the analysis of work absences in the individual departments. The localisation of the absentees may give an indication of a potentially workaholic superior or co-worker, as the absences may be motivated by a workaholic superior or co-worker. Moreover, other reasons for work absences are checked, which may affect the workaholic himself. Human resources management initially carries out a statistical evaluation on the following questions:

- How many employees were there with a corresponding frequency[31] (for example 3 x per year) of short-term illnesses? In this case, absences to a maximum of 3 days constitute short-term illnesses, irrespective of whether a medical certificate is provided.
- Which departments were they in?
- How many employees had long absences, for example longer than 14 days in a year?
- Which departments were they in?
- How many employees had no absences at all?
- Which departments were they in?

After the evaluation and processing of the figures, the next step is to check whether abnormalities can be detected in individual departments. If this is the case, before the departmental management is involved in the dialogue concerning the reasons for the work absences, the managers' behaviour should be checked for indications of workaholic behaviours, and if those behaviours might be the trigger for the absences within the group. This check may be conducted on the basis of personal experiences as well as all human resources instruments used within the company. Examples are strengths/weaknesses profiles in personnel information talks for management, personnel development appraisals, staff appraisals, or feedback through superiors. If workaholic traits have been detected in a manager, further action in accordance with a graduated escalation scheme[32] is recommended.

Notwithstanding the above, a dialogue on the clarification of the reasons for the absences between human resources management and the department is to be initiated and, if appropriate, conversations with those affected to be held.[33]

The diagnosis of absences based risk potential, when applied in a consistent and structured manner, is a useful instrument of work absences analysis, and is an efficient way to detect potential workaholism issues. In addition, it can be used as an early-warning system for possible departure or motivation risks.

---

31 The way criteria for analysis are determined is dependent on the intentions of the respective companies. At this point, only benchmarks are suggested.

32 The escalation level plan is presented in detail in Meißner 2005, S 204ff.

33 For comparison see the check-up interview in Meißner 2005, p. 217ff.

b) Fluctuation analysis

The targeted and structured fluctuation analysis is an instrument for researching the causes of employees' desire for change. Analogous to a work absences analysis, a regular statistical evaluation can show whether any department has specific abnormalities in regard to the fluctuation frequency. Building on that, further instruments, such as personnel information talk, staff assessments or the minutes of personnel development reviews, as well as personal experience, can help to determine whether there are indications of a workaholic employee or superior, which may have caused fluctuation amongst employees. In addition, supplementary personal conversations are necessary on the basis of a structured interview technique between human resources management and the employees changing roles in-house or externally, to get to the bottom of the reasons for the fluctuation. In this situation indicators directly pointing towards workaholism can be taken into account.

c) Assessment of management

This instrument is applied to evaluate managers along the company-specific management philosophy. The evaluation possibilities are manifold. The manager can be assessed by his direct superior, human resources management, or by the staff. A self-assessment is also feasible, or an external evaluation process, in which specific management criteria are assessed by professional trainers. When preparing the criteria, it makes sense to imply the relevant workaholism indicators (management behaviour, working style), to use these results for a later risk assessment.

d) Employee assessment

The instrument of regular employee assessments can be used for human resources risk management, in which superiors assess their employees about specific workaholism criteria to a certain degree of manifestation, and then this is analysed together with human resources management with regard to their risk potential. The criteria are discussed in conversation with the employees. In employee assessments, there is the opportunity, as in personnel information talks, to assess the potential and risk for every employee of the company.

6.1.4 Recommendation for the operational approach of a workaholism risk analysis

Figure 15 shows an example of how an operational human resources risk analysis in regard to workaholism could be meaningfully structured. An ideal

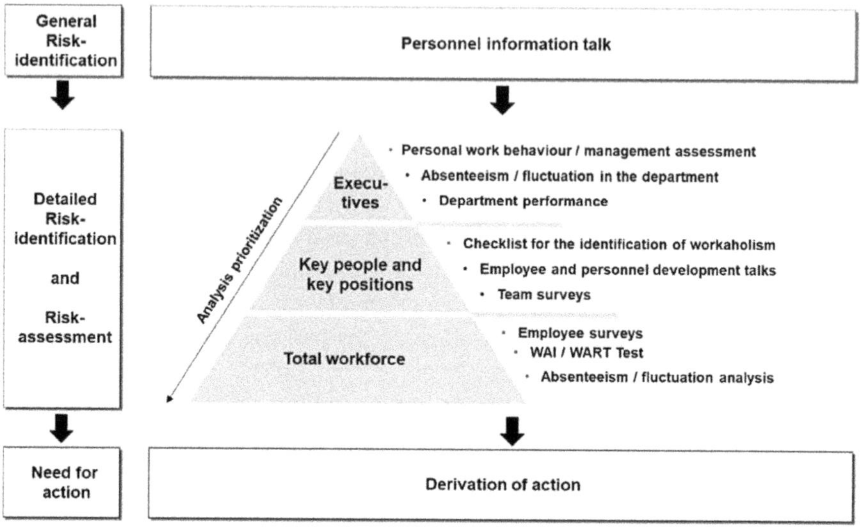

Figure 15: Development of company action guidelines
(Source: Own illustration)

introductory instrument is the personnel information talk, to gather all basic information on personnel and to gain a company-wide estimate on the current human resources risks. As the empirical study has shown, a tendency has emerged for certain risk groups. Even if the survey is not representative, and its findings are not valid, the results at least provide information on the possible order of a risk analysis, which indeed seems a viable introduction to the topic. The case studies have shown that managers are also affected by workaholism and suffer associated severe illnesses. These findings are also reflected in the personal experiences of the author, who has worked with workaholic managers in companies. As these doubtlessly take on an important position within a company, this group lends itself for the introduction of a risk analysis. The following points would be especially interesting in this examination:

- The personal work behaviour of the manager as well as management assessments
- Work absences and fluctuation within the department of the manager
- General departmental performance

Following would be the group of employees, who are either key personnel for the company or hold key functions. Key personnel and key functions mean in this context that, if this role is sub-optimally staffed or the position is vacant, this would cause disproportionately high economic damage to the company. The following instruments lend themselves here:

- Checklist for the identification of workaholism traits (see Table 22)
- Employee and human resources development interviews
- Team surveys

As a next step it seems useful to extend the risk analysis to all employees of the company. Here, the following instruments could be used:

- Employee surveys
- WAI/WART Test
- Analyses of work absences/fluctuation

Building on that, further investigations would follow, tailored to the abnormalities. Depending on the human resources risk, the following analysis will vary: if, for example, a high bottleneck risk is identified for a certain department, a specific work absences analysis should be carried out. In case of a high resignation risk, a fluctuation analysis, management feedback or a team survey would be suitable as tools for analysis.

The examples work absences and fluctuation analysis exemplify the interaction of the human resources instruments: Often, these instruments have already been implemented in companies, but are seen in isolation and not in an holistic context. The human resources risk analysis, together with the initial instrument of the personnel information talk, sheds a different light on the existing instruments, and interrelations become clear or are newly discovered.

As an alternative to the process described above, the examination results make it also sound feasible to attempt an age-group oriented risk analysis. As mapped out in Chapter 4.2.1., the age groups most significantly affected by workaholism were people aged from 41 – 50 years and 51 – 60 years. Within a proactive health management, one could begin with a targeted risk analysis, for example by utilising the WAI or WART test in these age groups, before extending the examination to all age groups.

6.2 Recommendations for action for management

As the analysis of management as to the development or promotion of workaholism has shown, managers play a central role in this: Managers, on the one hand, create the operational framework conditions and, on the other hand, they actively influence employees with their management behaviour.

Irrespective of the results of this study, the key role of the manager also becomes clear in the following recommendations/comments made by the participants in this study, which are here quoted in their original wording:

- *'Conversations, limitation of work hours, information about the addiction and about therapy options.'*
- *'Conversations; sympathy for my situation; defining appropriate/feasible applications together.'*
- *'To have my problems acknowledged.'*
- *'I received help: my employer has put me onto a professional career coach, who was also a trained therapist and who had my workaholism in her focus! That is great!'*
- *'Sandwich-Feedback: 'One' work method to be improved, packed between 'two' working methods that have been assessed as good, meaning a feedback on the areas someone is good at (not enough praise at the workplace).'*
- *'I would have wished for more understanding at my lowest point. In the meantime, my relationship with my employer has greatly improved and there is mutual trust.'*
- *'Transparent capacity planning.'*
- *'Knowledge about the topic of workaholism, conversations about personal problems through workaholism, education about co-dependency in nursing (in the social sector this is closely related to workaholism).'*
- *'Timely support by a further employee (not received despite request, or too late respectively. Burnout too far advanced at the time support was provided).'*
- *'Better internal organisation: I often went to work sick, as I knew that colleagues, who had been overtaxed already, had to fill in for me.'*
- *'Control over my overtime (350 hours of overtime), do not delegate all work to me, convert fixed-term contracts into permanent ones in order to reduce the pressure on the fixed term'*

Against this background, managers should be aware of their special responsibility and be specifically made aware of the workaholism issue.

a) Education on the workaholism issue

Management training offers a good opportunity to educate the participants on the topic of workaholism. Special emphasis should be laid on behavioural traits and symptoms. It should also be made clear which economic and human resources consequences a workaholic employee carries for the company and the department, and which influence the manager exerts or may exert on the promotion or development of workaholism respectively. Such training has the advantage of an employee being able to discuss the matter in a safe environment with like-minded people, and to overcome possible inhibitions, to talk about workaholism in general. Only a trusting and serious communication leads to a supposedly 'taboo topic' being discussed, and to possible problems being debated. This basic sensitising forms the basis for a further procedure in dealing with workaholism in companies.

On top of the training, a proactive information policy can be applied within the company, which offers employees the opportunity to take a self-test[34] and actively take advantage of support measures. These could be in the form of social counsellors or specially trained ombudspersons, with which those affected can discuss a recovery plan. Ombudspersons could be, for example, members of the workers' council.

b) Identification of workaholic behaviours

From a human resources point of view, the question is how to identify typical behaviours of workaholics. To that purpose, Table 21 divides workaholic behaviours into categories as to whether the ability of outsiders to detect them is easy, medium or hard. It also lists suitable instruments for the recognition of the respective behaviours traits.

Human behaviour implies an interaction, either with an outsider or with oneself. If the behaviour is oriented outwardly, it is easy to spot for outsiders. This includes outbursts of anger, mood and also work results not delivered by deadline. These characteristics are usually near-term and immediately detectable.

Some behaviours are assigned to the category 'medium', as it cannot be exactly defined here whether the behaviours are directed inwardly or outwardly. The point 'delegation' can be observed, when the affected person *must* delegate in line with his role, but does not do so. The behaviour is not observable if the affected person *could* delegate, but does not do so. In this case, the workaholic is in conflict with himself, without outsiders noticing. These behaviour traits can often become detectable by others after a longer period of time.

The characteristics in the 'hard' category are only hard to detect because the workaholic usually fights out these points with himself and the behaviour is oriented inwards. A manager will find it hard to determine whether an employee is interested in the work and in the outcome, or if employees make creative contributions. Generally, such behaviours only become obvious and observable after a longer period of time.

34 Self-test: Workaholics Anonymous, Work Addiction Risk Test, scale for workaholism.

Table 21: Identifiability of workaholic behaviour traits

Workaholic behavioural patterns	observability	Accountabilities/Instruments
They are the first to arrive each day & the last to leave	easy	Time stamp clock
They are moody	easy	M/Team
Work results are not submitted in time, for fear of them being faulty	easy	M: work results, deadlines
Collaboration in the team is inhibited, as they are constantly raising new concerns	easy	M: deadlines
They suffer outbursts of anger	easy	M/Team
An absolutely flawless quality of work is their work requirement	easy	M: work results
They are not a good team worker with an eye for what is essential	easy	M/Team
They take on tasks, although they do not have to	easy	M
They do not learn from mistakes	medium	M: work results
They take work home	medium	M: work results, email traffic, date file was saved
They also work weekends and while on holiday	medium	M: work results, email traffic, date file was saved
They seek new tasks, although old ones are not completed	medium	M: work results
Their day-to-day work is characterised by a hectic and uncoordinated style of work	medium	M
Small talk about private matters does not take place, as they are solely fixated on work	medium	M
They excessively control their colleagues/co-workers, because they do not trust them to be able to complete the tasks independently	medium	Team
They are not able to delegate tasks	medium	M
They do not take risks and also accept 80 %-solutions	medium	M: work results
They are not interested in the work/outcome	hard	M: work results
They do not make creative contributions	hard	M/Team
They do not tolerate work errors in others	hard	Team

(Source: Own illustration, M=manager)

Technology can only occasionally help here, as the examples 'they are the first to arrive each day and the last to leave', 'they take work home', 'they also work weekends and while on holiday' show. A time-recording system shows start and finish times, if the employee properly clocks in and out. This comes with the caution that the affected person, in order to conceal his addiction, may clock in later in the morning, but has actually started earlier, or clocks out in the evening, but stays on. Further to this, the manager should take note of the date and time on email traffic. With this, the working hours can be traced, and conclusions can be drawn as to excessive hours of work. Also, the date a file was saved can be used as an analytics tool, to get a picture of the work behaviour of an affected person.

The table clearly demonstrates that it is predominantly the manager who is able to identify the abnormal behaviour traits of workaholics. For the sake of completeness, it will be stated here again that these are not recommendations for the control of all employees, but that these are measures which can be used to gain insights into an individually affected person who has shown abnormal work behaviours, where one would like to analyse whether workaholism could be present or not.

A valid measuring instrument for management is the analysis of work results:

- Are these too perfect and did they take by far too long to complete them?
- Have they been delivered on time?
- Can a learning curve be identified, if mistakes have been made?
- Were team results not handed in on time?

From the assessment of work results, a manager can gather many valuable clues, as to whether workaholism may be present in the employee displaying such abnormalities.

Beyond that, it is primarily the level of empathy within management, and the careful observation of the company's own employees, that form prerequisites for the detection of workaholic behaviour. This become evident in the examples 'they take on tasks, although they do not have to', 'a hectic and uncoordinated style of work characterises their day-to-day work', 'small talk about private matters does not take place, as they are solely fixated on work', which can only be detected if managers are sustainably and attentively showing an interest in the employees beneath them, and pay close attention to them and care for them.

Moreover, certain traits can be found mainly in teams, as the examples 'they are not a good team worker with an eye for what is essential', 'they excessively control their colleagues/co-workers, because they do not trust them to be able to complete the tasks independently', 'they do not tolerate work errors in others'

Table 22: Checklist for the identification of features of workaholism in employees

Name:____________________ **Workaholism – Criteria**	**Evaluation yes/no**	**Notes**
Working hours:		
Working hours within the operational requirements		
No or normal availability after work		
No or only occasional work from home/on holiday/on weekends		
Overtime within the operational guidelines		
Work behaviour:		
Adherence to timeframes		
Quality of results meets expectations		
Normal frequency of queries		
Normal personal work requirements		
Tasks not/hardly begun, without old ones having been finished		
Learning from mistakes		
Style work is calm and coordinated		
80 % of solutions are accepted		
Teamwork:		
Interaction within the team is inconspicuous		
Behaviours (moods, outbursts of anger) are inconspicuous		
Team members are not conspicuously controlled		
Tasks are delegated appropriately		
Makes a creative and productive contribution to the team		
Own work errors and those of others are tolerated		
Absences:		
Number of days		
Reasons		
Key functions		
Academic training:		
Age		
Difficult operational framework conditions:		

(Source: Own illustration)

show. For abnormal behaviours to be openly addressed by a team, it needs a very open, trusting and fear-free culture of discussion within the team, which should be created by the manager, as the team leader. If this culture does not exist, those affected will be automatically involved in an openly fought out or covert conflict, which would inevitably inhibit the work productivity of the team.

To get a feeling for the workaholism issue among their employees, managers can utilise the checklist for the identification of workaholism traits (see Table 22). The more traits that are ticked as 'no', the higher the probability that the evaluated employee may suffer from workaholism issues. Sometimes there is a situation in which managers sense that 'something' is not right with their employee, without being able to put it into words. This missing determinability of ills is typical for a situation involving workaholism. The checklist may help to give clarity. Building on that, further steps can be initiated. To look at the operational framework conditions is the next step of the analysis, in which the extent to which operational influences may be the cause for workaholic behaviours is examined.

If a manager were to identify an abnormality in relation to the team, the next step would be the analysis and questioning of the team. The manager should, at this point, also face team feedback, to reflect on his own behaviour regarding workaholism inducing or promoting framework conditions. Whether this is to be investigated in the form of an open team discussion, or an anonymous team survey, depends on the prevailing trust culture and on the size of the group. This process requires sensitivity and maybe an external moderator who guides the team and the manager through it.

The team questions can be deduced from the checklist for the identification of workaholism, and extended by the appropriate point from Chapter 4.2.2. 'operational Influences'.

7 Summary and outlook

The economic and human resources focussed approach to qualitative research on the issue of workaholism was mainly possible due to the comprehensive description of individual case studies through Robinson and Fassel, who, with their research, have provided a detailed picture of workaholism. The intention of this research work continues that of the 2005 study and comprised these three focal points:

1. An explorative empirical study of the workaholism issue from the perspective of affected workaholics.
2. A risk analysis in connection with workaholism.
3. Pragmatic action guidelines for instruments to assess human resources risks as well as for management.

The current study was carried out against the background of two objectives:

One objective of the empirical study was the analysis of workaholism indicators (symptoms, characteristics and types of workaholism), the investigation of workaholism inducing and promoting operational influences, as well as the listing of potential economic and especially human resources risks associated with workaholism on an individual business level.

The second objective was a comparison with the 2005 study, in which the same questions were examined, although the target group of those surveyed had then been human resources managers, whereas in the current study those affected by workaholism themselves were the test subjects. It was to be determined whether the findings from back then could be confirmed from the point of view of those affected.

The current study confirms the findings of the 2005 study for the operational handling of workaholism:

- Workaholism is fundamentally an addiction issue carrying high economic and human resources risks for companies.
- Even if medical acceptance is officially lacking, a consideration in human resources risk management seems appropriate.
- In the case of abnormal work absences, fluctuation, or motivation issues, workaholism should be involved in the analysis and checked as a potential causal factor.

The empirical research in this study has led to the following conclusions:

- The high number of workaholics in dependent employment should be a clear indicator for companies that they, with high probability, can expect to have workaholic individuals among their employees. Companies should approach this responsibility and this risk with an accordingly structured human resources risk management, to identify those affected, and to support them in a goal-oriented fashion.
- People with an academic degree make up a slightly larger risk group in this study.
- Especially the case studies have shown that this group has more managers with long term illnesses. They should be prioritised in the risk assessment, as they are generally key persons for companies and, thus, carry the corresponding responsibility for the achievement of corporate goals.
- The low level of work absences among the test subjects indicates that companies should not neglect the analysis of short-term illnesses when carrying out a workaholism risk assessment and to probe for more detail, to learn more about the causes for the work absences.
- The symptoms of workaholism can clearly be divided into two groups in this study: the group >50 % mainly displays symptoms that do not tend to need medical attention, whereby the symptoms < 50 % are more likely to need medical treatment. This makes the identification of workaholism harder for companies, because these can only be identified through observable behaviour.
- The analysis of symptoms seems to affirm that the test subjects of this study as participants of Workaholics Anonymous meetings tend to display less serious illnesses. From this, the importance of the prophylactic work of Workaholics Anonymous can be inferred.
- The fears described in the 2005 study of employees, with regard to operational framework conditions, were confirmed in the current study as workaholism inducing factors.
- Companies, managers and human resources departments should be aware that practised corporate culture and management behaviour may cause general fears in employees, and may also promote the development of workaholism. According to this survey, this especially applies to the organisation of the operational framework conditions. The behaviour of managers plays a key role here: Managers, on the one hand, have a hand in creating the operational framework conditions and, on the other hand, actively exert influence on the employees through their management behaviour and, thus, also on the development or promotion of workaholism. This hereby confirms the prioritisation of risk analysis towards managers.

The risk analysis of this study focussed on the following topics:

- Risk analysis of workaholic behavioural patterns
- Risk analysis of symptoms of workaholism
- Risk analysis of operational influences on the development or promotion of workaholism respectively

The following findings could be gained from the study:

- The following economic and human resources risks were identified:
  - Delay of work processes
  - Unfinished tasks
  - Deadline delays
  - Controlling behaviour towards colleagues
  - Mistakes
  - Wrong decisions
- These risks are overall abnormalities which should be able to be detected by managers or colleagues. This led to the discovery of further indicators, which could be used for the detection of workaholic employees in companies.
- With this result, the current study makes it clear that workaholic behavioural patterns in companies occur with a corresponding probability and may at 70 % pose a medium to high risk for companies.
- 33% of the symptoms constitute a high risk potential for companies, whereby even 24 % of which are visible from the outside. Overall, 62 % of the workaholism symptoms can be allocated to a medium to high risk potential. These numbers clearly indicate the necessity for a straight forward illnesses analysis in companies, in order to verify these risks and to initiate the appropriate action measures for the reduction of these risks.
- The risk portfolio of operational influences on the development or promotion of workaholism again emphasised the specific responsibilities of managers. This underlines the recommendation to look urgently at managers in the prioritisation planning for risk analyses.

Recommendations for action:
With the human resources risk analysis instruments, the following opportunities in regard to workaholism were closely looked at and their application discussed:

- Employee surveys
- Personnel information talks
- Work-Ability-Index
- Work Addiction Risk Test

- Analysis of absenteeism
- Fluctuation analysis

With regard to managers, emphasis is on the importance of information and the training of superiors as to workaholism traits, in order to soften the 'taboo subject' of workaholism, and to develop a culture of trust. Moreover, the study has identified the necessity for management to develop a system as to how the observed behaviours of employees (for example unrest, tension, mood swings, irritability/ impatience, exhaustion, forgetfulness, hyperactivity) may be analysed. For this purpose, a checklist was created, which should make it easier for managers to identify typical workaholic behaviours and traits.

In conclusion, this study has shown, by means of a number of materials, that workaholics can be identified by observed behaviours and visible symptoms, but that due to the lack of identification instruments, a high number of unidentified cases of workaholism can be assumed to be present in companies. This again becomes clear in Figure 16, in which the corporate phases of workaholism, which have been discussed in Chapter 1, are once more symbolically represented as an iceberg. Phases 1 and 2 run subliminally, workaholics act and operate in the operational environment increasingly with larger effects and risks. They are not detected as workaholics and represent an undefinable hidden number for the business.

Only after workaholism openly comes to light, which often occurs as a serious illness of the affected person, is a company forced to take appropriate measures and to act. In Phase 3, a crisis stage may have been reached already and severe economic damage might have been done.

This, again, emphasises the great need for professional risk management.

Also this study still stands at the beginning of workaholism research in the German speaking world. To improve the basis for further investigations, medical, social and economic recognition of the addiction is desirable. Further human resources areas of research could include the following questions:

- To what extent can incurred costs be measured, which have actually been caused by workaholics and how can a concrete risk evaluation be carried out?
- To what extent can decreased work results caused by workaholic behaviours be measured? What could be the measurement criteria?
- To what extent can a reduced ability to perform caused by the symptoms of workaholic people be measured (such as disrupted sleep), which do not lead to work absences?

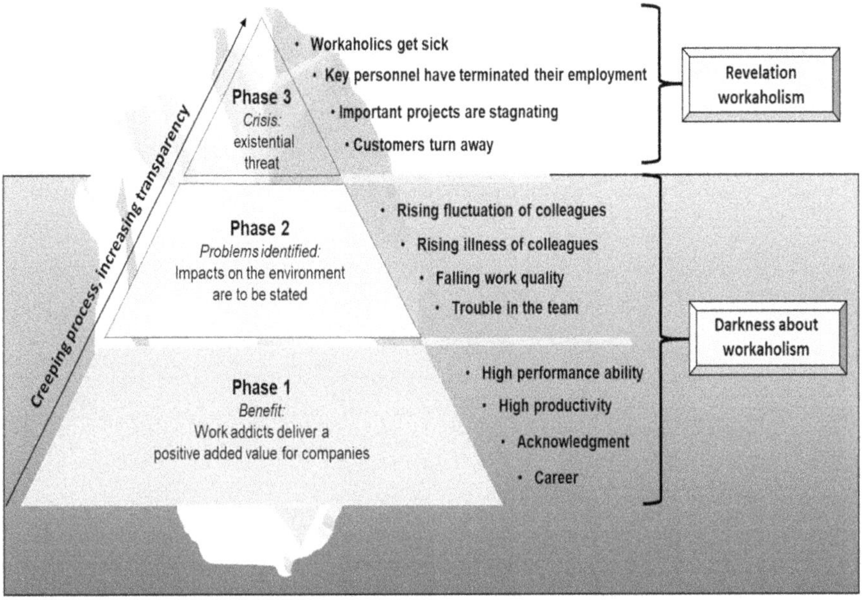

Figure 16: Operational escalation phases of workaholism
(Source: Own illustration)

The areas of scientific research on the topic of workaholism are extensive, and must be explored further. The aim of this work was to further exemplify the far-reaching issue of workaholism from an economic and human resources perspective. The denial of the issue poses a risk which may threaten the existence of companies.

Companies should have the objective to recognise the issue of workaholism as an illness, to avert economic damage from the businesses and to actively approach the problems of their employees. Apart from human resources risk management, this could be in the form of pro-active strategies, for example as part of the company health management, developed together with management, to sustainably maintain their employees' ability to work, ensure a humane work environment, and to offer support to workaholics in their fight against the illness and help them regain a normal attitude towards work.

Bibliography

AAS Anonyme Arbeitssüchtige, internet: www.arbeitssucht.de, Workaholics Anonymus, internet: http://www.workaholics-anonymous.org/.

Ackermann, Karl-Friedrich (1999), Risikomanagement im Personalbereich. Reaktion auf die Anforderungen des KonTraG, Wiesbaden, Gabler Verlag.

Badura, Bernhard et al (2013), Fehzeiten-Report, Berlin, Heidelberg, Springer Verlag.

Berger, Peter (2002), Arbeitssucht. Psychotherapie von Arbeitssucht. Vortrag an der Universität Leipzig, 8. Psychologiestudierenden Kongress am 30. November 2002, www.hardtwaldklinik2.de/home/informationen.html.

Berger, Peter (2014), Wenn Arbeiten zur Krankheit wird, 9. Basler Frühjahrstagung am 04.04.2014, https://www.wicker.de/fileadmin/user_upload/HWK_2_Hardtwaldklinik_2/Downloads/Arbeitssucht-Wenn-arbeiten-zur-Krankheit-wird.pdf.

Bielert, Svea (2009), Arbeitssucht – was sich hinter dem Phänomen verbirgt und welche präventiven Maßnahmen der betrieblichen Gesundheitsförderung in deutschen Unternehmen durchgeführt werden, Diplomarbeit Leuphana Universität Lüneburg.

Bitz, Horst (2000), Risikomanagement nach KonTraG, Stuttgart, Schäffer-Poeschel Verlag.

Büchner, Uwe (1993), Sucht als artifizielle Ich-Funktion. Ich-psychologische Suchttheorien. In: Bilitza, Klaus Walter (1993) Suchttherapie und Sozialtherapie. Psychoanalytisches Grundwissen für die Praxis. Göttingen/Zürich, Vandenhoeck & Ruprecht.

Fassel, Diane (1990), Working ourselves to death: The high cost of workaholism and the rewards of recovery, San Francisco, Harper Collins Publishers.

Fassel, Diane (1994), Wir arbeiten uns noch zu Tode. Die vielen Gesichter der Arbeitssucht, München, Droemersche Verlagsanstalt Th. Knaur Nachf.

Fergen, Andrea / Pickshaus Klaus (2001), Arbeitszeit und Gesundheit. In: Pickshaus, Klaus, Schmitthenner, Horst, Urban, Hans-Jürgen (2001), Arbeiten ohne Ende. Neue Arbeitsverhältnisse und gewerkschaftliche Arbeitspolitik, Hamburg, VSA-Verlag.

Füser, Karsten (1999), Risikomanagement (KonTraG) – Erfahrungen aus der Praxis. In: Der Betrieb, 52. Jg. (1999), S. 753–758.

Gerke, Wolfgang (2003), Das Pflichtenheft des Risikomanagements. In: Frankfurter Allgemeine Zeitung Nr. 98 vom 28.04.2003, S. 26.

Giefer, Katrin (2003), Personalrisiken werden unterschätzt. In: GIT Sicherheit und Management 07/2003 S. 22–24.

Glißmann, Wilfried (1999), Neue Selbständigkeit in der Arbeit, Ökonomik der Maßlosigkeit und die Frage der Gesundheit. Aufsatz im Rahmen eines Workshops des Forums Arbeitsschutz (Verbundprojekt im Auftrag des Bundesministeriums für Forschung und Bildung) in Dresden.

Gross, Werner (1990), Sucht ohne Drogen. Arbeiten, Spielen, Essen, Lieben..., Frankfurt am Main, Fischer Taschenbuch Verlag GmbH.

Heide, Holger (1999), Arbeitssucht - Skizze der theoretischen Grundlagen für eine vergleichende empirische Untersuchung. Beiträge zur sozialökonomischen Handlungsforschung. SEARI. Universität Bremen.

Heide, Holger (2000), Inidividual and social economic dimensions of work addiction. Beiträge zur sozialökonomischen Handlungsforschung. Nr. 4. SEARI. Universität Bremen. (Vortrag im Rahmen der Fachtagung 'Sucht 2000' der Dt. Hauptstelle gegen die Suchtgefahren in Karlsruhe).

Hochrein, Karen (1999), Das Gesetz zur Kontrolle und Transparenz im Unternehmensbereich (KonTraG) und die Folgen für das Personalmanagement. In: Ackermann, Karl-Friedrich (1999), Risikomanagement im Personalbereich. Reaktion auf die Anforderungen des KonTraG, Wiesbaden, Gabler Verlag.

Jungkurth, Caroline (2005), Arbeitssucht in Deutschland? Geschäftstüchtig, Berlin, Logos Verlag.

Karmasin, Fritz / Karmasin Helene (1977), Einführung in Methoden und Probleme der Umfrageforschung, Wien, Köln, Graz, Hermann Böhlaus Nachf.

Kobi, Jean-Marcel (2002a), Personalrisikomanagement – Strategien zur Steigerung des People Value, Wiesbaden, Gabler Verlag.

Kobi, Jean-Marcel (2002), Die Früherkennung von Personalrisiken als Pflicht. In: Personalmagazin 10/2002, S. 20–21.

Lück, Wolfgang (1998), Elemente eines Risiko-Managementsystems. Notwendigkeit eines Risiko-Managementsystems durch den Entwurf eines Gesetzes zur Kontrolle und Transparenz im Unternehmensbereich (KonTraG). In: Der Betrieb, 51. Jg. (1998), S. 8–14.

Lamnek, Siegfried (1995), Qualitative Sozialforschung. Methodologie (Band 1) sowie Methoden und Techniken (Band 2), München, Psychologie-Verlag-Union.

Matthey, Linda (2011): Arbeitssucht unter Journalisten. In: Badura, Bernhard et al (2013): Fehzeiten-Report, Berlin, Heidelberg, Springer Verlag.

Mentzel, Gerhard (1979), Über die Arbeitssucht. In: Zeitschrift für psychosomatische Medizin und Psychoanalyse. Jg. 25., S. 115–137.

Nieder, Peter (1999): Fehlzeiten- und Fluktuationsrisiken: Erfassung, Bewertung, Abbau. In: Ackermann, Karl-Friedrich (1999), Risikomanagement im Personalbereich. Reaktion auf die Anforderungen des KonTraG, Wiesbaden, Gabler Verlag.

Meißner, Ulrike (2005), Die 'Droge' Arbeit, Unternehmen als Dealer und als Risikoträger, Personalwirtschaftliche Risiken der Arbeitssucht, Frankfurt am Main, Peter Lang Verlag.

Meißner, Ulrike (2017), Unternehmensrisiko Arbeitssucht – Managementherausforderungen und Aktionsleitfaden für die Praxis, Frankfurt am Main, Peter Lang Verlag.

Niebling, Gottfried G., (1997), Die Suchtgesellschaft. Zur Soziogenese eines Phänomens 'individueller' Pathologie, Aachen, Verlag Mainz, Wissenschaftsverlag.

Oellerking, Claus (2002), Selbsthilfegruppen für Arbeitssucht. In: Heide, Holger (2002), Massenphänomen Arbeitssucht. Historische Hintergründe und aktuelle Entwicklung einer neuen Volkskrankheit, Bremen, Atlantik-Verlag.

Pickshaus, Klaus / Schmitthenner, Horst / Urban, Hans-Jürgen (2001), Arbeiten ohne Ende. Neue Arbeitsverhältnisse und gewerkschaftliche Arbeitspolitik, Hamburg, VSA-Verlag.

Pitsch, Rainer (2002), Innere Kündigung erkennen und gegensteuern. In: Personalwirtschaft 11/2002, S. 55–57.

Poppelreuter, Stefan (1996), Arbeitssucht: Integrative Analyse bisheriger Forschungsansätze und Ergebnisse einer empirischen Untersuchung zur Symptomatik, Witterschlick/Bonn, Wehle.

Richter, Hans-Jürgen (1969), Grundlagen schriftlicher Massenbefragungen. Ein verhaltenstheoretischer Beitrag zur Methodenkritik, Dissertation an der Ludwig-Maximilians-Universität München, Druck: Janikowski.

Richter, Bernd / Gößmann, Sabine / Steinmann, Horst (1984), Arbeitssucht im Unternehmen. Zur Genese und personalwirtschaftlichen Konsequenzen. Lehrstuhl für allg. BWL und Unternehmensführung der Universität Erlangen-Nürnberg, Prof. Dr. Horst Steinmann, Diskussionsbeiträge Heft 24.

Robinson, Bryan E. (2000), Wenn der Job zur Droge wird. Ein Leitfaden für Workaholics, ihre Partner, Kinder und Therapeuten, Düsseldorf/Zürich, Walter Verlag.

Robinson, Bryan (2014), Chained to the desk: a guidebook for workaholics, their partners and children, and the clinicians who treat them, New York and London, New York University Press.

Sandjaja, Yen (2007), Wenn aus dem Job eine Sucht wird, Saarbrücken, VDM Verlag Dr. Müller.

Schneider, Christian, (2001), Skala für Arbeitssucht, Veröffentlichung im Internet: https://opus.bibliothek.uni-wuerzburg.de/files/168/schneider.pdf.

Schwochow, Rainer (1997), Workaholics – Wenn Arbeit zur Sucht wird, Berlin, Christoph Links Verlag.

Spence, J. T.; Robbins, A.S. (1992), Workaholism: Definitions, Measurement and Preliminary Results. In Journal of Personality Assessment, 58, S. 160–178.

Städele, Michaela (2008), Arbeitssucht und die zwanghafte Persönlichkeitsstörung, Saarbrücken, VDM Verlag.

Statistisches Bundesamt (2016), Krankenstand, Veröffentlichung im Internet: https://www.destatis.de/DE/ZahlenFakten/Indikatoren/QualitaetArbeit/Dimension2/2_3_Krankenstand.html.

Statistisches Bundesamt, (04/2017), Verbraucherpreisindizes für Deutschland, Veröffentlichung im Internet: https://www.destatis.de/DE/Publikationen/Thematisch/Preise/Verbraucherpreise/VerbraucherpreisindexLangeReihen PDF_5611103.pdf?__blob=publicationFile.

Stigler, Huber (2001), Skriptum Methodologie, http://www-gewi.kfunigraz.ac.at/edu/studium/materialien/meth.doc.

Temple, Jürgen/Ilmarinen, Juhani (2013): Arbeitsleben 2025, Hamburg, VSA Verlag.

Uhl, Alfred (1997), Probleme bei der Evaluation von Präventionsmaßnahmen im Suchtbereich. In: Wiener Zeitschrift für Suchtforschung, Jg. 20, 1997, Nr. 3+4, S. 93–109.

Vicario, Christina (2013), Arbeitssucht im helfenden Dienstleistungssektor, Veröffentlichung im Internet: https://www.katho-nrw.de/fileadmin/primaryMnt/KatHO/DISuP/Masterthesen/Masterthesis_CVicario_2013.pdf.

Voigt, Christine (2006), Arbeitssucht, Persönlichkeitsmerkmale von Arbeitssüchtigen und prägende Rollenmodelle, Saarbrücken, VDM Verlag.

Wilson Schaef, Anne /Fassel, Diane (1994), Suchtsystem Arbeitsplatz. Neue Wege in Berufsalltag und Management, München, DTV.

Wolf, Sabine (2002), Geschlechtsspezifische Suchtproblematik – Ein unverzichtbarer Baustein für ein ganzheitliches Verständnis der Arbeitssucht. In: Heide, Holger (2002), Massenphänomen Arbeitssucht. Historische Hintergründe und aktuelle Entwicklung einer neuen Volkskrankheit, Bremen, Atlantik-Verlag.

Sources case studies

Berlin.de (*2015*), Arbeitssuchterkennen und Hilfe finden, http://www.berlin.de/special/gesundheitundbeauty/gesundheit/psychologie/16119422260865 arbeitssuchterkennenundhilfefinden.html.

b:place balance (*2015*), Arbeitssucht als unerkannte Falle, http://www.arbeitssucht.ch/fallbeispiel.php.

ZEIT ONLINE (*2015*), Abhängigkeit: Süchtig nach Arbeit, http://www.zeit.de/wissen/gesundheit/201002/arbeitssucht/komplettansicht.

Lange, Jennifer (*2016*), NDR Info: Wenn der Job zur Sucht wird, https://www.ndr.de/ratgeber/gesundheit/Wenn-der-Job-zur-Sucht-wird,arbeitssucht102.html.

Henes-Karnahl (*2006*), Workaholismus: Kein Kavaliersdelikt, sondern eine (Sucht-) Krankheit, LexisNexis Deutschland GmbH, Newsletter 04/2006, S. 10–12.

Kramer, Bernd (*2015*), Leben eines Workaholics, Spiegel Online, http://www.spiegel.de/karriere/berufsleben/workaholics-500-000-menschen-sind-suechtig-nacharbeit-a-1007645.html.

Sperlich, Christel (*1995*), Berliner Zeitung, Workaholics zerstören mit der Sucht nach Erfolg und Macht auch die Familie / Therapie kann Teufelskreis durchbrechen: 'Nur wenn ich arbeite geht die Angst weg', http://www.berliner-zeitung.de/workaholics-zerstoeren-mit-der-sucht-nach-erfolg-und-macht-auch-die-familie---therapie-kann-teufelskreis-durchbrechen--nur-wenn-ich-arbeite--geht-die-angst-weg--17391834.

Pfersdorf, Silke, Schweitzer, Arnd (*2008*), 'Die Arbeit war meine Droge, der Gedanke an Urlaub machte mich nervös', in Stern Nr. 4, S. 104.

Rudzio, Kolja (*2016*), Die unbekannte Sucht, in: ZEIT Nr. 19, 28.04.2016, http://www.zeit.de/2016/19/workaholic-sucht-arbeit-anonyme-arbeitssuechtige.

Wild, Beate (*2011*), Der Job als Droge, in Süddeutsche Zeitung Nr. 266, 18.11.2011.

Express (*2013*), Workaholics Wie erkenne ich die Anzeichen für Arbeitssucht?, in Express 15.10.2013 http://www.express.de/ratgeber/gesundheit/-workaholics-wie-erkenne-ich-die-anzeichen-fuer-arbeitssucht--22907000.

Schaller, Vivianne (*2016*), Workaholismus/Arbeitssucht, FHS St. Gallen, https://elearning.fhsg.ch/mod/wiki/viewversion.php?pageid=147&versionid=615.

Spiegel, Monika (*2015*), Tüchtig und süchtig, Wiener Zeitung, http://www.wienerzeitung.at/themen_channel/wz_reflexionen/vermessungen/740461_Tuechtig-und-suechtig.html?em_cnt_page=2.

Auer, Matthias, Höller, Christian (*2015*), Wenn die Arbeit zur Sucht wird, Die Presse, http://diepresse.com/home/wirtschaft/economist/4674340/print.do.

Trappe, Thomas (2014), Nichts als Arbeit, Human Resources Manager, http://www.humanresourcesmanager.de/ressorts/artikel/nichts-als-arbeit-10627.

Bundesverband Deutscher Internisten e.V. (2010), Arbeiten bis zur Erschöpfung, http://www.internisten-im-netz.de/de_aktuelle-rheuma-meldungen_1772_0_983_arbeiten-bis-zur-ersch-pfung-aus-sucht.html.

Kals, Ursula (2009), Tüchtig oder süchtig?, Frankfurter Allgemeine Zeitung, http://www.faz.net/aktuell/beruf-chance/arbeitswelt/workaholics-tuechtig-oder-suechtig-1783233.html?printPagedArticle=true#pageIndex_2.

Vitte, Stanley (2007), Wenn Arbeit zur Sucht wird, FOCUS Online, http://www.focus.de/finanzen/karriere/berufsleben/worklife/tid-7397/workaholics_aid_132617.html.

www.ingramcontent.com/pod-product-compliance
Ingram Content Group UK Ltd.
Pitfield, Milton Keynes, MK11 3LW, UK
UKHW020152290926
15471UKWH00005B/829

9 783631 766347